# INTERACTING WITH HISTORY

# INTERACTING WITH HISTORY

*Teaching with Primary Sources*

EDITED BY KATHARINE LEHMAN

An imprint of the American Library Association
CHICAGO 2014

Printed in the United States of America

18  17  16  15  14        5  4  3  2  1

Extensive effort has gone into ensuring the reliability of the information in this book; however, the publisher makes no warranty, express or implied, with respect to the material contained herein.

ISBN: 978-0-8389-1205-8 (print).

**Library of Congress Cataloging-in-Publication Data**

Interacting with history : teaching with primary sources / edited by Katharine Lehman.
    page cm.
    Includes bibliographical references and index.
    ISBN 978-0-8389-1205-8 (alk. paper)
    1.  Library of Congress. Teaching with Primary Sources Program. 2.  United States—History—Study and teaching. 3.  United States—History—Sources. 4.  History—Study and teaching. 5.  History—Sources.  I. Lehman, Katharine B., author, editor of compilation.
E175.8.I57 2014
973.071—dc23                                                                    2013044197

Cover design by Kimberly Thornton. Images courtesy of the Library of Congress.
Text design in The Janson Text and Brandon Grotesque typefaces by Alejandra Diaz.

♾ This paper meets the requirements of ANSI/NISO Z39.48-1992 (Permanence of Paper).

# Contents

# Acknowledgments

S pecial thanks to Kathy McGuigan and Stephen Wesson in the Educational Outreach Department of the Library of Congress for their help and support in this project. With the encouragement and assistance of the Educational Outreach staff and the participants of the 2011 Library of Congress Summer Institute willing to share their successful lesson plans, this resource embodies the full depth and richness of the study of primary sources that we strive to provide.

This book would never have gone to print without the expertise of the three main contributors, Sherrie Galloway, Sara Suiter, and Mary Alice Anderson, who have exceptional experience teaching primary sources at the Library of Congress and in university courses. I am ever grateful to Barbara Stripling for agreeing to introduce our work with her superior understanding of the nature and importance of studying primary sources. Personal thanks also to Gail Petri, my hostess and guide while attending the Library of Congress Summer Institute, who encouraged me to undertake this editing project.

In chapter 4, eight educators contributed lessons that have been described and duplicated for sharing. They are: Teresa St. Angelo, a kindergarten teacher from John I. Dawes—Early Learning Center in Manalapan-Englishtown, New Jersey; Jennifer Burgin, a third-grade teacher at Oakridge Elementary School, part of Arlington Public Schools in Arlington, Virginia; Sandy Rodeheaver, a traveling resource teacher in Garrett County Public Schools in Oakland, Maryland; Krista McKim, a middle school English teacher in Montgomery County Public Schools, Maryland; Carrie Veatch, an online high school history teacher in Colorado; Victoria Abens, the librarian at the Academy of Notre Dame, grades 6–12, in Villanova, Pennsylvania; Esther Kligman-Frey, a teacher trainer for the San Francisco Museum of Modern Art, who carries lessons to schools and conferences in the San Francisco Bay area and across California. All lesson contributors—including the compiler of chapter 4, Katharine Lehman, who also contributed a lesson—successfully completed a Summer Institute at the Library of Congress in 2011.

From all the contributors of chapters and lessons, this book is our gift to students and teachers. Combining our knowledge and love of the subject, we have detailed multiple strategies and examples of how primary sources can be used in professional development and in classrooms. We hope all who read this volume will come away with a deeper understanding of the powerful catalyst these resources can be to help students "observe, question, and reflect" about history and apply lessons learned to events in the present and in the future.

KATHARINE LEHMAN, EDITOR

# Introduction

BARBARA K. STRIPLING

Freshman year in high school. One spring day—a special showing of a World War II documentary with news footage of the liberation of concentration camps. And thus I was propelled into a lifetime passion for understanding the Holocaust through the eyes of those who experienced it.

Primary sources do indeed have the authenticity and power to bring history to life. Not every encounter with a primary source will have the profound effect that the images from World War II had on my life, but when students connect with the voices and images of real people from the past, they start to see the story behind the litany of facts and events presented in many history textbooks.

Primary sources are defined by the Library of Congress as objects and documents that were created at the historical time, as opposed to secondary sources that have been created to interpret, evaluate, or summarize firsthand evidence. Through digitization, the Library of Congress and other organizations (e.g., libraries, museums, archives) are building robust repositories of primary sources in multiple formats, including moving images, photos, government documents, letters, audio recordings, maps, and publications. Increasingly, students and teachers have access to primary source evidence of history, albeit digital facsimiles rather than the actual artifacts.

As K–12 educators reimagine their instruction to integrate the teaching of critical thinking and literacy skills across the curriculum (as outlined in the Common Core State Standards), the benefits of using primary sources in all classrooms will become increasingly evident. Primary sources were created in the course of living, not to teach about living during that time period. As a result, they present authentic glimpses into historical events, decisions, and people—moments in time representing specific points of view. Further, students are intellectually challenged to analyze the perspective underlying each primary source and interpret its effect on the information presented.

In fact, analyzing point of view is only one of the thinking skills fostered by the use of primary sources. Because the sources themselves do not tell the reader/viewer what to think but must be critically examined and interpreted, primary sources open the door to inquiry. They provoke questioning, engagement, and exploration of the incomplete pictures they present. Students are drawn to make inferences to fill in the gaps and are propelled to check their inferences through deeper investigation; they then form their own conclusions based on the evidence they have collected and interpreted.

Just as primary sources lead to inquiry, so too they offer powerful opportunities for teaching critical literacy skills. Since historical primary sources were created for authentic purposes in response to particular situations or events, they tend to be complex "texts" that can be interpreted only with an understanding of the historical language and context. Educators guide students to probe the vocabulary and use of language within the text to understand the meaning. To help students deepen their understanding of any underlying meaning, teachers and librarians provide background information (often through the use of secondary sources) and present a variety of primary sources created from different perspectives.

Helping students analyze and interpret primary sources in context leads to another important strength of using primary sources: the development of historical empathy. Historical empathy is a complex construct that involves the cognitive ability to understand an attitude, action, or decision in context—to understand the "why" of history without judging based on current values and hindsight. Some history researchers also include within the definition of historical empathy the concept of emotive empathy, or the ability to identify and understand the feelings of participants without attempting to "share" the emotions. When students confront historical actions and decisions, and have an understanding of the environment that led to those actions, they are able to empathize with the decision maker, even if they do not agree with the decision from their twenty-first-century perspective. Primary sources enable students to see the people behind history; that connection to the people who created the sources and to the pressures and conflicts that they faced leads to the development of an empathetic view, and therefore a deeper understanding of history.

The use of primary sources is not without its challenges. Unless students are taught to apply critical thinking and inquiry skills to every primary source—even the seemingly easily accessible ones such as photographs—students will gather only superficial impressions of meaning rather than deeper historical understanding. Photographs become mere illustrations instead of specific evidence of a particular moment in time and place. Diaries become generalizations that represent the story of everyone who lived at the time, with no attention paid to the reasons for the actions and thoughts of the particular writer.

The challenge to teach students to use primary sources well during historical inquiry is also a golden opportunity for librarians and classroom teachers to teach the skills that are embedded in library information skills curricula and the Common Core State Standards. All educators know that these thinking-process skills are essential for successful academic and personal learning and success in college and career. The instructional partnership between classroom teachers and librarians to design instruction that integrates process skills with content and incorporates a wide variety of both primary and secondary sources has never been more important.

Designing instruction to take advantage of the profound benefits of using primary sources is complicated, and most educators are not prepared to embark on this journey. Although institutions such as the Library of Congress have developed robust websites to provide guided access and support for educators, the organized and strategic use of primary sources requires an understanding of what sources are available, how to gather and organize them for use in the classroom and library, how to teach students to analyze and interpret them, and how to integrate the resources into historical inquiry units.

This book provides answers to those challenges. Each chapter addresses issues with valuable information and practical advice, detailing specific sources and strategies that will make the use of Library of Congress resources effective for engaging students in developing deep understanding of history. In the first chapter, educators are offered an overview of primary sources and the Library of Congress. Later chapters provide specific guidance on the wealth of primary sources available through the Library of Congress; strategies to design effective instruction with primary sources (including information about the professional development tools and resources available on the LOC website); examples of units and lessons designed by educators across the country; and finally, support for teaching students to discover local sources of history.

Dive in, engage, and enjoy learning the magical power of primary sources to transform the educational experience of your students. Perhaps you will create the experience that inspires a lifelong passion for learning and fosters historical empathy and understanding in each of your students.

# Welcome to the Library of Congress

SHARON METZGER-GALLOWAY

The Library of Congress is a treasure trove of incredible collections of primary sources. Many digital collections are available to learners whether they come to Washington in person or visit online. Let's take a look at what this amazing institution has to offer.

## HISTORY

When the United States government moved from Philadelphia to Washington City in 1800, a congressional library was established and housed in the new Capitol building. This library was primarily a law library when the Capitol burned during the War of 1812. (It is believed this devastating fire on August 24, 1814, began in this library.) While Washington stood in ruins, Thomas Jefferson offered to sell his personal library to Congress. After much debate, the purchase of 6,487 volumes was completed for the agreed-upon sum of $23,950. Jefferson allowed Congress to decide on the price, but he stipulated that the collection must be purchased in its entirety. The collection was diverse and many in Congress felt they did not need books on art, architecture, medicine, and so on. Jefferson argued, "I do not know that it contains any branch of science which Congress would wish to exclude from their collection; there is, in fact, no subject to which a member of Congress may not have occasion to refer."[1] Once the purchase was completed, the precedent was set for the Congressional Library to continue to collect, preserve, and share a comprehensive universal and diverse collection.

FIGURE 1.1
Aerial View of Capitol Hill
Featuring the Library of Congress
Thomas Jefferson Building
behind the US Capitol.
Photograph by Carol Highsmith.
Library of Congress Prints and
Photographs Division.

FIGURE 1.2
View of the Library of Congress
Thomas Jefferson Building
from the US Capitol Dome.
Photograph by Carol Highsmith,
Library of Congress Prints
and Photographs Division.

Topped with a sculpted golden torch of knowledge, a new separate facility—known today as the Thomas Jefferson Building—was completed in 1897 across the street from the Capitol. This magnificent structure is often described as a temple to knowledge and human understanding; it is considered by some to be the most beautiful building in Washington, restored to its original grandeur in 1997 (figs. 1.1, 1.2, and 1.3). A trip to our nation's capital would not be complete without a visit to the Library of Congress. For those unable to make it in person, virtual tours of the building are available online, as well as its vast digital collections.

## ONLINE TOURS

What does the Library of Congress website have to offer to the virtual visitor?

Begin your exploration at www.loc.gov and follow the path to the visitor's section from the main page (fig. 1.4). Select "Visit the Library" for highlights of many areas of interest to online visitors.

**Concerts, Lectures, and Other Events.** Public events such as booktalks, poetry readings, lectures, and live concerts are highlighted in this section of the website and cover a wide array of topics and interests; many are available shortly after the event via webcasts. These webcasts, which have been recorded since 2001, include talks given by many authors who visit the library each year for individual events and authors who present at the National Book Festival. Students and teachers will be thrilled to see and hear some of their favorite authors talk about their writing process, their inspirations and the back stories of their books. A full list can be found by entering the keyword *webcasts* in the search box.

**Tours.** There are several self-guided tours of the beautiful buildings and all the ornate decorations available, too. Explore the Jefferson Building with the virtual tour available online or with a special iTunes app easily downloaded to your computer or mobile device. "Take an online tour" will allow you to focus on many special features more closely online than you can in person. See the murals by John White Alexander that illustrate the Evolution of the Written Word. Click through each section to see details of paintings and sculptures throughout the Jefferson Building; particularly noteworthy is the spectacular center dome of the Main Reading Room.

**More Guided Tours.** This section highlights the many things to do at the library, including scheduling tours for individuals, groups, and students. Links to the online exhibitions and schedules of gallery talks lead you to interesting showcases of the library's diverse collections. Note: No preview is available.

**Exhibitions.** Featured exhibitions give visitors an opportunity to view items from the many collections of the Library of Congress in person or online. Once an exhibition has closed, the online version continues to be accessible in the "All Exhibitions" section of the website.

FIGURE 1.3
Library of Congress, Capitol Domes. Photograph by Carol Highsmith. Library of Congress Prints and Photographs Division.

FIGURE 1.4
Screen capture of the "Visiting the Library" page of the Library of Congress website showing links for online virtual tours and events.

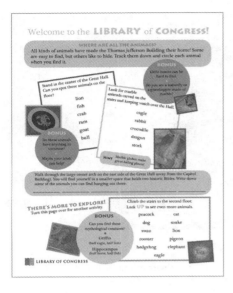

FIGURE 1.5
Children's *Welcome to the Library of Congress* activity sheet.

FIGURE 1.6
Great Hall. View from the Second Floor West Corridor.
Library of Congress Thomas Jefferson Building.
Photograph by Carol Highsmith. Library of Congress
Prints and Photographs Division.

(See examples of lesson plans and teacher materials available for use with these exhibitions in chapter 2.)

## LIBRARY OF CONGRESS ACTIVITY SHEETS FOR KIDS AND FAMILIES

Over the years, the mission of the Library of Congress has grown beyond providing resources for scholars and the members of Congress. A PDF printable guide to explore the Jefferson Building is geared toward children and helps them learn some of the history and fascinating facts about the architecture and exhibitions (fig. 1.5). In addition to exhibits geared for school-age children, there is an on-site Young Readers Center available on the ground floor of the library, with books and programming of interest to children and young adults.

## TAKE A VIRTUAL TOUR OF THE JEFFERSON BUILDING

Online visitors can explore the exterior details of the 1897 Library of Congress building. Ethnological heads—thirty-three faces representing various ethnic races from around the world—circle the first floor above each of the windows. On the second floor of the front facade, nine great men are memorialized with busts framed by round windows. A dramatic fountain featuring King Neptune and many mythological sea creatures greets visitors from the First Street sidewalk.

When you are ready to open the doors to see what is inside, the Great Hall (fig. 1.6) is the first space you enter.

The Jefferson Building has spectacular public spaces —including the Great Hall, decorated in the Beaux Arts style (fig. 1.7).

These carved marble cherubs, or putti, decorate the stairway to the second floor. Each depicts a vocation, such as gardener, entomologist, student, printer, mechanic, hunter, engineer, or chemist. These details are highlighted in the online tour of the Great Hall. Sculptures depicting lifelong learning top the main archway leading the way toward the center of the building. Elaborate stained glass covers the ceiling with a colorful geometric design.

## A LESSON FROM THE GODDESS OF WISDOM

The impressive mosaic of Minerva created by Elihu Vedder gazes down on visitors from the east side of second floor (fig. 1.8). She portrays the Roman goddess of wisdom, who is at peace.

Allowing students to take a closer look at these details is part of a classroom activity available through the "Teacher Resources" pages. "The Minerva Mosaic of the Library of Congress" lesson (fig. 1.9) was developed by the library's Educational Outreach team for intermediate and middle grades. It guides students through a basic analysis of the symbolic elements from Greek and Roman mythology.

FIGURE 1.7
Philip Martiny's Carvings on the Stair. The figures depict a gardener with a spade and watering jar, an entomologist with a butterfly net, a reading student wearing a mortarboard, and a printer with type and a press. Photograph by Carol Highsmith. Library of Congress Prints and Photographs Division.

FIGURE 1.8 (Top)
Great Hall. [View of Second Floor with Minerva in Distance.] Photograph by Carol Highsmith. Library of Congress Prints and Photographs Division.

FIGURE 1.9 (Right)
Minerva in the Great Hall. Photograph by Carol Highsmith. Library of Congress Prints and Photographs Division.

**LIBRARY OF CONGRESS TOUR COMPANION LESSON PLANS**

**Evolution of the Book: Introducing Students to Visual Analysis**
- www.loc.gov/teachers/classroommaterials/lessons/book

**The Minerva Mosaic of the Library of Congress**
- www.loc.gov/teachers/classroommaterials/lessons/minerva/procedure.html

**The Thomas Jefferson Building: Secret Messages**
- www.loc.gov/teachers/classroommaterials/presentationsandactivities/jefferson.html

FIGURE 1.10
Main Reading Room.
[View from Above Showing
Researcher Desks.
Library of Congress
Thomas Jefferson Building,
Washington, DC.]
Photograph by Carol Highsmith.
Library of Congress Prints
and Photographs Division.

## THE READING ROOM

One of the most spectacular features of the Jefferson Building is found below the golden torch: the Main Reading Room (fig. 1.10). This inspirational space is circled with symbolic plaster and bronze portrait statues, as well as stained-glass windows depicting the forty-eight states and territories at the time the building was constructed.

A painting at the top of the dome lantern ceiling represents human understanding (fig. 1.11). Circling the base of the lantern is the Blashfield Collar, a mural representing twelve areas that contributed to modern civilizations. (For more information on the dome art, see the library docent training webcast "The Blashfield Collar and Lantern Medallions.")

There are other galleries and pavilions with elaborate decorations, paintings, murals, and mosaics. Each section has a theme, such as the Family Gallery or Poetry Gallery, and includes symbolic mosaics and murals. Each corner pavilion includes sculptures and murals that can be explored in depth as well.

There are several formats for the touring the Jefferson Building online. The first is accessed via the "Visit the Library" section of the main page (www.loc.gov/visit). There is a virtual tour app available through iTunes. This tour gives you options to visit various locations in the Jefferson building as well as several of the exhibitions. These tour options include photographs and information about the individual rooms and spaces of this building.

FIGURE 1.11
Main Reading Room. [Interior of Dome. Library of Congress Thomas
Jefferson Building, Washington, DC.]
Photograph by Carol Highsmith. Library of Congress Prints
and Photographs Division.

## EXHIBITIONS

Visitors can take a virtual tour of the current exhibits on display. Also note that current exhibits and all past exhibits are online and available for teachers with full explanations for classroom study.

## ALL EXHIBITIONS

The west side of the Jefferson Building has gallery spaces where many of the library's exhibitions are displayed. Some of the exhibits are ongoing, while others are open for a specific length of time. Fortunately, past exhibitions are digitized and available for online exploration long after they have physically closed (www.loc.gov/exhibits/all; fig. 1.12). These collections and their curatorial information are a treasure trove for the classroom. Currently there are over one hundred exhibits digitized for browsing. Many of the items in these exhibits come from the library's extensive collections, much of which is available without restrictions for classroom use.

Recent exhibits may also include "Special Presentations." These interactive multimedia presentations are available in multiple formats and bring artifacts to life for the viewer with zoom features and activities for learners of all ages. Browse the exhibition sections and dig deeper into the collections and topics. A "Learn More" tab on each exhibit page will take you to resources for the classroom, as well as suggested titles for further reading. Look for references to teacher workshops or institutes under "Resources for Teachers." This section highlights resources organized under themes that are geared for classroom use.

## CREATING THE UNITED STATES

The *Creating the United States* exhibition (fig. 1.13) focuses on the formation of a self-governing United States of America—specifically, creating the Declaration of Independence, the Constitution, and the Bill of Rights. This collection of original documents, letters, maps, newspapers, and political cartoons demonstrates the compromises and collaborations of the process.

FIGURE 1.12
Screen capture of the "All Exhibitions" page from the Library of Congress website.

FIGURE 1.13
Screen capture of the exhibition *Creating the United States*. Library of Congress.

One of the more popular "Special Presentations" shows the original Rough Draft of the Declaration of Independence penned by Thomas Jefferson (fig. 1.14). This four-page, handwritten document was created in secret and when the committee came together many changes were made. In the online interactive feature, select "overview" to explore each page of this document. From this view you can see a transcription of the original document and identify where each crossed out edit was made and the new version that evolved. You can also click on themes such as "Pursuit of Happiness" to explore "Where Did This Idea Come From" to view antecedent documents where certain phrases may have originated. A similar format for all versions will give students background information on these important founding documents.

All these resources are available in high resolution and can be displayed in the classroom. In the "Learn More" section, a collection of teacher resources is available and includes high-resolution PDFs that were created for teacher institutes held in conjunction with the exhibit. Where possible, each item is linked to the document's online home, its location in the exhibit, a PDF, and a transcription, if available. Analysis tools and guides for teachers are also available in PDF format for reproduction.

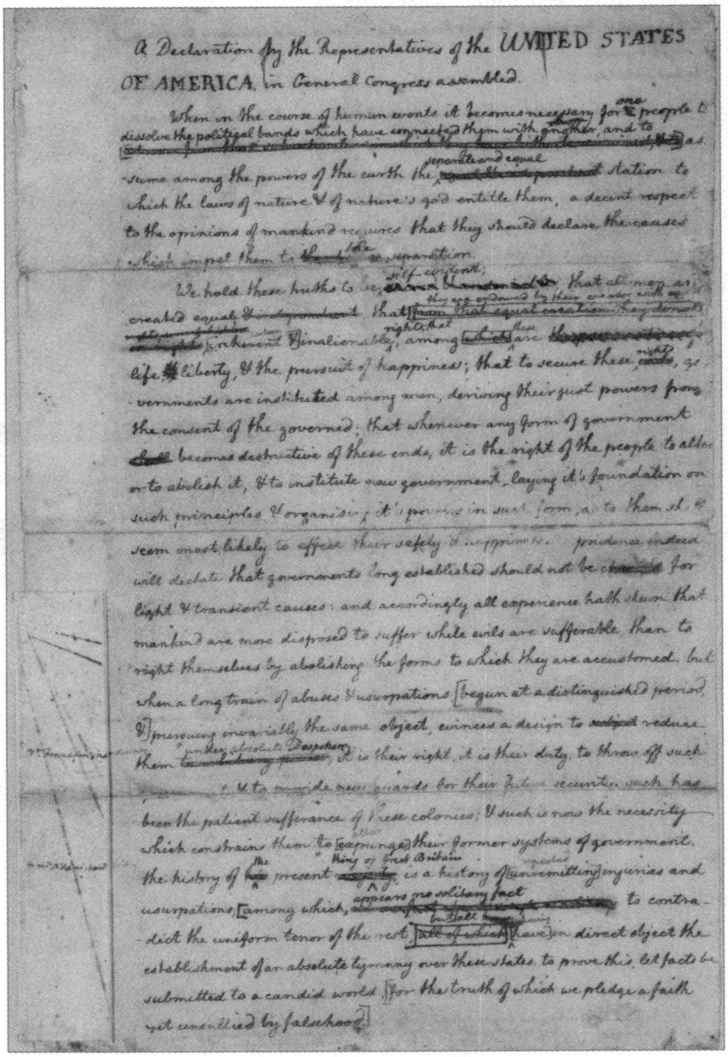
A Declaration by the Representatives of the UNITED STATES OF AMERICA, in General Congress assembled.

When in the course of human events it becomes necessary for one people to dissolve the political bands which have connected them with another, and to assume among the powers of the earth the separate and equal station to which the laws of nature & of nature's god entitle them, a decent respect to the opinions of mankind requires that they should declare the causes which impel them to the separation.

We hold these truths to be self-evident; that all men are created equal; that they are endowed by their creator with ... inherent & inalienable rights; that among these are life, liberty, & the pursuit of happiness; that to secure these rights, governments are instituted among men, deriving their just powers from the consent of the governed; that whenever any form of government becomes destructive of these ends, it is the right of the people to alter or to abolish it, & to institute new government, laying it's foundation on such principles & organising it's powers in such form, as to them shall seem most likely to effect their safety & happiness. prudence indeed will dictate that governments long established should not be changed for light & transient causes: and accordingly all experience hath shewn that mankind are more disposed to suffer while evils are sufferable than to right themselves by abolishing the forms to which they are accustomed. but when a long train of abuses & usurpations [begun at a distinguished period, & pursuing invariably the same object, evinces a design to reduce them under absolute Despotism, it is their right, it is their duty, to throw off such government & to provide new guards for their future security. such has been the patient sufferance of these colonies; & such is now the necessity which constrains them to [expunge] their former systems of government. the history of the present King of Great Britain is a history of [unremitting] injuries and usurpations, [among which, appears no solitary fact to contradict the uniform tenor of the rest, but all have] in direct object the establishment of an absolute tyranny over these states. to prove this, let facts be submitted to a candid world [for the truth of which we pledge a faith yet unsullied by falsehood]

FIGURE 1.14
Draft of the Declaration of Independence showing edits penned by Thomas Jefferson. Library of Congress.

---

*CREATING THE UNITED STATES* **COMPANION LESSON PLANS INCLUDE**

**The Declaration of Independence: From Rough Draft to Proclamation**
- www.loc.gov/teachers/classroommaterials/lessons/declaration

**The Constitution: Drafting a More Perfect Union**
- www.loc.gov/teachers/classroommaterials/lessons/more-perfect-union

**The Bill of Rights: Debating the Amendments**
- www.loc.gov/teachers/classroommaterials/lessons/bill-of-rights

---

## EXPLORING THE EARLY AMERICAS

The *Exploring the Early Americas* exhibition (fig. 1.15) includes highlights from the Jay I. Kislak Collection of artifacts from the native cultures of the Americas ("Pre-Contact"), documentation and evidence once the European encounter took place ("Exploration and Encounters"), and finally the consequences of this merging of peoples ("Aftermath of the Encounter"). The library's existing collections help tell the story of the rich culture of the Mayas, the Aztecs, and the Incas. It also traces the motivation and the consequences of European exploration and settlement, along with the impact this had on the indigenous cultures. The resulting aftereffects are evidenced in the art, maps, letters, and documentation of this extraordinary time in history.

This exhibition includes "Special Presentations" that allow viewing of sculptures, vases, decorative items, and other artifacts (fig. 1.16). Some items have webcasts of well-known historians explaining the current understandings about these items. A series of paintings called the Conquest of Mexico has zoom features to explain segments each of the six paintings in detail.

FIGURE 1.15
Screen capture of the exhibition *Exploring the Early Americas*.
Library of Congress.

FIGURE 1.16
Vase with Deer Hunting Procession.
Photograph by Justin Kerr. Jay I. Kislak
Collection, Rare Book and Special
Collection Division. Library of Congress.

FIGURE 1.17
Universalis Cosmographia
Secunda Ptholemei Traditionem
Et Americi Vespucci
Aliorum Que Lustrations
[1507 Map Showing America].
Map by Martin Waldseemüller.
Geography and Map Division,
Library of Congress.

One of the top treasures of the Library of Congress is also available from the "Aftermath of the Encounter" section of this exhibition, the Waldseemüller Map from 1507 (fig. 1.17). This was the first known map to have a land mass labeled America. It also shows this land as a separate continent and depicts a new ocean (now known as the Pacific). This map is often referred to as "the birth certificate of America." Webcasts and narrative explain the significance of this treasure and help viewers look at important details.

Teacher workshops have been offered at the library, and additional resources are available for the educator in the "Learn More" section. Links to lesson plans, activities, and webcasts—as well as the "Teacher Institute Resource Materials" gallery of reproducible items—give the classroom access to many of the items from the exhibit. These collections include lessons on maps, vases, and other artifacts.

---

### EXPLORING THE EARLY AMERICAS COMPANION LESSON PLANS INCLUDE

**Huexotzinco Codex**
- www.loc.gov/teachers/classroommaterials/lessons/codex

**Drake's West Indian Voyage 1588–1589**
- www.loc.gov/teachers/classroommaterials/lessons/drake

**Waldseemüller's Map: World 1507**
- www.loc.gov/teachers/classroommaterials/lessons/waldseemuller

**Maps and Mapmakers: Seeing What's on the Map**
- www.loc.gov/teachers/classroommaterials/presentationsandactivities/maps.html

## WITH MALICE TOWARD NONE

Even though some exhibitions have closed, many of the rich items are still available to view online. *With Malice Toward None*, the exhibition celebrating the two hundredth anniversary of Lincoln's birth, is one such example (fig. 1.18). Many of the items come from the library's Lincoln collections, but some items are on loan from private collectors. The focus of this exhibit is on Lincoln's rise to national prominence, his presidency, and his assassination.

Teacher workshops have been offered at the library, and additional resources are available for the educator in the "Learn More" section, with lesson plans, activities, webcasts, and a gallery of select items for reproduction. There are original speeches, transcripts, and prints depicting the First and Second Inaugural addresses, the Gettysburg Address, and the Emancipation Proclamation. Samples of political cartoons, maps, and sheet music are included, as well the letters exchanged between Lincoln and eight-year-old Grace Bedell, where they discuss whether Lincoln should grow a beard (see chapter 3 for a lesson based on the exchange between Lincoln and Bedell).

## THOMAS JEFFERSON'S LIBRARY

Thomas Jefferson's library, which was purchased by Congress in 1814, established the core of the Library of Congress for the future. The vast collections we have available today began with the 6,487 volumes purchased for $23,950. Though many of the originals have been destroyed, exact duplicates fill out the exhibition *Thomas Jefferson's Library* (fig. 1.19). Jefferson organized his collection into three categories: Memory, Reason, and Imagination. This is still a working collection, but the display allows for access to any needed volumes.

The exhibition follows Jefferson's categories and explores some of the individual books and their significance to him. Online links to the exhibition overview, exhibition items, public programs, special presentations, and resources for teachers can be found on the website www.loc.gov/exhibits/thomas-jeffersons-library/index.html.

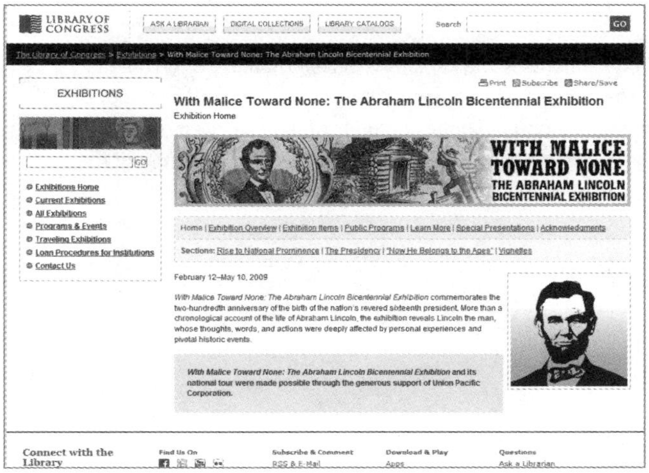

FIGURE 1.18 (Bottom left) Screen capture of the Lincoln exhibition *With Malice Toward None*. Library of Congress.

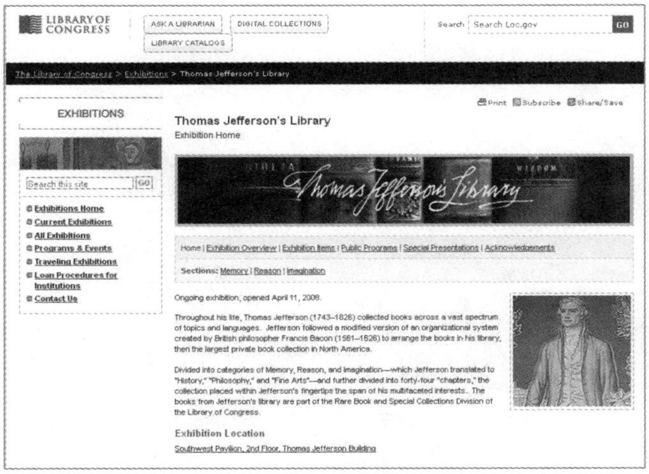

FIGURE 1.19 (Bottom right) Screen capture of the *Thomas Jefferson's Library* exhibition. Library of Congress.

Jefferson's love of knowledge and legacy to the Library of Congress and the American people is explained on the library website:

> Throughout his life, books were vital to Thomas Jefferson's education and well-being. When his family home Shadwell burned in 1770 Jefferson most lamented the loss of his books. In the midst of the American Revolution and while United States minister to France in the 1780s, Jefferson acquired thousands of books for his library at Monticello. Jefferson's library went through several stages, but it was always critically important to him. Books provided the little traveled Jefferson with a broader knowledge of the contemporary and ancient worlds than most contemporaries of broader personal experience. By 1814 when the British burned the nation's Capitol and the Library of Congress, Jefferson had acquired the largest personal collection of books in the United States. Jefferson offered to sell his library to Congress as a replacement for the collection destroyed by the British during the War of 1812. Congress purchased Jefferson's library for $23,950 in 1815. A second fire on Christmas Eve of 1851 destroyed nearly two thirds of the 6,487 volumes Congress had purchased from Jefferson.[2]

---

### THOMAS JEFFERSON'S LIBRARY COMPANION LESSON PLANS

**Thomas Jefferson's Library: Connecting the Books to the Life**
- www.loc.gov/teachers/classroommaterials/presentationsandactivities/jefferson-library.html

  In these activities appropriate for grades 4–12, students are asked to match actual books in Jefferson's collection to roles he filled in his life such as architect, inventor, scholar, scientist and leader.

**Thomas Jefferson's Library: Making a Case for a National Library**
- www.loc.gov/teachers/classroommaterials/lessons/jefferson

  The overview for the lesson states:
  *Students examine a letter written by Thomas Jefferson and identify techniques he used to persuade Congress to purchase his personal library. Students consider a selection of Jefferson's books and then write their own persuasive letters urging the books' purchase, while considering the question: "Why would Congress need this book to shape or govern the nation?"*

  *Included among the lesson plan documents is the persuasive letter Thomas Jefferson sent to Samuel Smith extolling the need for members of Congress to research information in all areas. The letter is presented in its original handwritten form and is transcribed for students to read more easily. A graphic organizer is provided for students to apply the principles learned from Jefferson's argument to their own persuasive argument.*

---

Source: "Lesson Plan: *Thomas Jefferson's Library: Making a Case for a National Library*," Library of Congress, accessed July 20, 2013, www.loc.gov/teachers/classroommaterials/lessons/jefferson.

## SUMMARY

Browsing the Library of Congress's website can take visitors on a virtual tour of the art and architectural spaces of this magnificent building. Exploring the webcasts and recorded events can be the next best thing to being there in person. Teachers will discover lesson plans accompanying exhibits and architectural features as well as the primary source material stored in the collections. Delving deeper into the exhibitions past and present, guests will begin to grasp the depth and breadth of the treasures to be discovered for learners of all ages.

## NOTES

1. "Thomas Jefferson's Letter to Samuel H. Smith," letter from Thomas Jefferson, September 21, 1814, in *The Works of Thomas Jefferson in Twelve Volumes*, federal edition, collected and edited by Paul Leicester Ford.
2. "*Thomas Jefferson:* Overview," exhibition overview, Library of Congress, accessed March 10, 2012, www.loc.gov/exhibits/jefferson/overview.html.

## BIBLIOGRAPHY—WEBSITES

Alexander, John W. *Evolution of the Written Word*. Thomas Jefferson Building—Online Tours Library of Congress. 2014. Accessed April 8, 2014. www.loc.gov/visit/tours/online-tours/thomas-jefferson-building.

*Creating the United States: Creating the Declaration of Independence*. Creating the Declaration of Independence (Library of Congress). Accessed April 8, 2014. www.loc.gov/exhibits/creating-the-united-states/interactives/declaration-of-independence.

*Creating the United States*. Exhibitions (Library of Congress). 2014. Accessed April 8, 2014. www.loc.gov/exhibits/creating-the-united-states.

*Exhibition Overview—Thomas Jefferson's Library* (Library of Congress Exhibition). Exhibitions—Thomas Jefferson (Library of Congress). Accessed March 10, 2012. www.loc.gov/exhibits/jefferson/overview.html.

*Exploring the Early Americas. Conquest of Mexico Paintings*. Conquest of Mexico Paintings (Library of Congress). Accessed April 8, 2014. www.loc.gov/exhibits/exploring-the-early-americas/interactives/conquest-of-mexico-paintings.

*Exploring the Early Americas*. Exhibitions (Library of Congress). 2014. Accessed April 8, 2014. www.loc.gov/exhibits/exploring-the-early-americas.

*Exploring the Early Americas. Waldseemüller Maps*. Waldseemüller Maps (Library of Congress). Accessed April 8, 2014. www.loc.gov/exhibits/exploring-the-early-americas/interactives/waldseemuller-maps.

Highsmith, Carol M. *Aerial View of Capitol Hill Featuring the Library of Congress Thomas Jefferson Building behind the U.S. Capitol, Washington, DC*. Digital image, 2007. Library of Congress Prints and Photographs Division. Accessed March 3, 2012. www.loc.gov/pictures/item/2007683665.

————. *Great Hall*. [Detail of Putti (Gardner, Entomologist, and Student) on Grand Staircase, *Philip Martiny, Sculptor. Library of Congress Thomas Jefferson Building, Washington, DC.*] Digital image, 2007. Library of Congress Prints and Photographs Division. Accessed March 3, 2012. www.loc.gov/pictures/item/2007684281.

————. *Great Hall. View from the Second Floor West Corridor. Library of Congress Thomas Jefferson Building, Washington, DC*. Digital image, 2007. Library of Congress Prints and Photographs Division. Accessed March 3, 2012. www.loc.gov/pictures/item/2007684267.

————. *Great Hall. View of Second Floor with Minerva in Distance. Library of Congress Thomas Jefferson Building, Washington, DC*. Digital image, 2007. Library of Congress Prints and Photographs Division. Accessed March 3, 2012. www.loc.gov/pictures/item/2007687181.

————. *Library of Congress, Capitol Domes, Washington, DC*. Digital image, 1980–2006. Prints and Photographs Division Library of Congress. Accessed March 3, 2012. www.loc.gov/pictures/item/2011630583.

————. *Library of Congress Minerva Mosaic in the Great Hall of the Thomas Jefferson Building, Washington, DC*. Digital image, 1980–2006. Library of Congress Prints and Photographs Division. Accessed March 3, 2012. www.loc.gov/pictures/item/2011630706.

————. *[Main Reading Room. Interior of Dome. Library of Congress Thomas Jefferson Building, Washington, DC.]*. Digital image, 2007. Library of Congress Prints and Photographs Division. Accessed March 4, 2012. www.loc.gov/pictures/item/2007684369.

————. *Main Reading Room. [View from above Showing Researcher Desks. Library of Congress Thomas Jefferson Building, Washington, DC.]* Digital image, 2007. Library of Congress Prints and Photographs Division. Accessed March 4, 2012. www.loc.gov/pictures/item/2007687187.

————. *View of the Library of Congress Thomas Jefferson Building from the U.S. Capitol Dome, Washington, DC*. Digital image, 1980–2006. Library of Congress Prints and Photographs Division. Accessed March 3, 2012. www.loc.gov/pictures/item/2011632501.

Jefferson, Thomas. "Declaration of Independence Rough Draft."—*Exhibitions (Library of Congress)*. Accessed April 8, 2014. www.loc.gov/exhibits/creating-the-united-states/creating-the-declaration-of-independence.html.

Kerr, Justin I. *Vase with Deer Hunting Procession*. Digital image. Exhibition Items—*Exploring the Early Americas*. Exhibitions (Library of Congress). Accessed April 8, 2014. www.loc.gov/exhibits/exploring-the-early-americas/interactives/reading-pre-columbian-artifacts/items/item-9-large.html.

"Lesson Plan: Thomas Jefferson's Library: Making the Case for a National Library." Thomas Jefferson's Library. Accessed March 10, 2012. www.loc.gov/teachers/classroommaterials/lessons/jefferson.

"Meet the Authors." National Book Festival Teens & Children's Author Webcasts. 2014. Accessed April 8, 2014. www.loc.gov/bookfest/kids-teachers/authors.

*The Minerva Mosaic of the Library of Congress Lesson Overview*. The Minerva Mosaic of the Library of Congress. Accessed March 4, 2012. www.loc.gov/teachers/classroommaterials/lessons/minerva/index.html.

*The Minerva Mosaic of the Library of Congress Procedure*. The Minerva Mosaic of the Library of Congress. Accessed March 4, 2012. www.loc.gov/teachers/classroommaterials/lessons/minerva/procedure.html.

Samuels, Anne. *Blashfield Collar and Lantern Medallions*. Lecture, Library of Congress Webcast, Washington, DC, November 2, 2006. Accessed April 8, 2014. www.loc.gov/today/cyberlc/feature_wdesc.php?rec=4258.

Sharpe, David. *Jefferson's Library Recreated for the Thomas Jefferson Exhibition—(Library of Congress Exhibition)*. Digital image. Thomas Jefferson—Exhibitions—(Library of Congress). Accessed March 10, 2012. www.loc.gov/exhibits/jefferson/jefflib.html.

"Thomas Jefferson's Letter to Samuel H. Smith." Letter from Thomas Jefferson. September 21, 1814. In *The Works Of Thomas Jefferson in Twelve Volumes. Federal Edition. Collected and Edited by Paul Leicester Ford*. Accessed September 16, 2012. www.loc.gov/teachers/classroommaterials/lessons/jefferson/pdf/letter.pdf.

*Thomas Jefferson's Library*—Exhibitions. Exhibitions (Library of Congress). 2014. Accessed April 8, 2014. www.loc.gov/exhibits/thomas-jeffersons-library.

"Tours & Activities." Library of Congress Home. Accessed July 22, 2013. www.loc.gov/visit/tours.

Waldseemuller, Martin. *Universalis Cosmographia Secunda Ptholemei Traditionem Et Americi Vespucci Aliorum Que Lustrations [1507 Map Showing America]*. Digital Image. *Exhibition Items—Aftermath of the Encounter—Exhibitions—(Library of Congress)*. Geography and Map Division, Library of Congress. Accessed April 8, 2014. www.loc.gov/item/2003626426.

*Welcome to the Library of Congress Activity Sheet*. Washington, DC: Library of Congress, 2011. Accessed April 8, 2014. www.loc.gov/portals/static/visit/documents/LOC-Animal-Worksheet.pdf.

*With Malice Toward None: The Abraham Lincoln Bicentennial Exhibition*. Exhibitions (Library of Congress). 2014. Accessed April 8, 2014. www.loc.gov/exhibits/lincoln.

# Teaching Resources from the Library of Congress

SARA SUITER

"So if this is a library, where are all the books?" During my year at the Library of Congress as the Teacher-in-Residence I heard this question asked on more than one occasion. Sometimes it came from local students participating in the library's LOC Box school program, but more than once I heard the question asked by visitors as they stood in the Great Hall of the Thomas Jefferson Building.

A short visit to the Main Reading Room or a stroll through one of the library's exhibits soon reveals the magnitude of the Library of Congress collection. With nearly 142 million items and one of the largest bodies of high-quality, digitized content available at www.loc.gov, those who may never come to Washington can gain access to the treasures of the nation's library.

Prior to joining the Educational Outreach team, I taught third grade in a dual-language immersion public charter school in Washington, DC. When I first started teaching, I soon realized that any background research to support my instructional planning would need to be conducted in the evenings or on the weekends—there was simply not enough time in the school day.

Attending a Library of Congress teacher institute transformed my teaching. In addition to discovering the key entry points for researching the library's digitized collections, I learned where to find ready-to-use classroom materials on the "Teachers" page and strategies for using primary sources in my instruction.

I started the following school year with hundreds of high-quality, engaging primary sources and ideas for using them at my fingertips. Whether using a photograph or a map, my students made connections between the details they noticed in the primary source and their prior knowledge. Each hypothesis they made was supported by evidence they observed. By focusing on three skills—observing, reflecting, and questioning—each student was given the opportunity to notice details and connect what they saw with their prior knowledge. In a class of mostly English Language Learners, this meant my former students were not constrained by content knowledge, and therefore felt confident enough to take risks.[1]

**FIGURE 2.1**
Screen capture of the "Teachers" entry page of the
Library of Congress website.

This chapter is an effort to share my knowledge of the Library of Congress "Teachers" page and its vast resources for teachers and school librarians.

## LIBRARY OF CONGRESS TEACHERS PAGE RESOURCES

The Library of Congress "Teachers" page (fig. 2.1) provides a range of resources for teachers that promote teaching with primary sources. Classroom materials available on this page provide easy access to the most relevant primary sources from the library's collections, making research and planning more efficient. The content is created and managed by the Educational Outreach team at the Library of Congress—comprised of former teachers, school librarians, and education specialists. The "Teachers" page should be the first stop in any search for primary sources. The Educational Outreach staff selects primary sources from across the Library of Congress collections that will engage students, develop critical thinking skills, and enable students to build new knowledge. Each curated set of primary sources provides links to additional resources on the Library of Congress website. Starting at the "Teachers" page allows teachers to focus their search on topics commonly covered in K–12 standards, and then expand their search to larger Library of Congress digitized collections.

## THEMED RESOURCES

The Educational Outreach team created "Themed Resources" in order to gather all "Teachers" page classroom materials on selected curricular themes in one place. If you are looking for primary sources on a particular topic, start by scanning "Themed Resources." Each themed resource contains links to other classroom materials on the same topic, covering subject matter in American history including advertising, flight and early aviators, and the Great Depression (fig. 2.2).

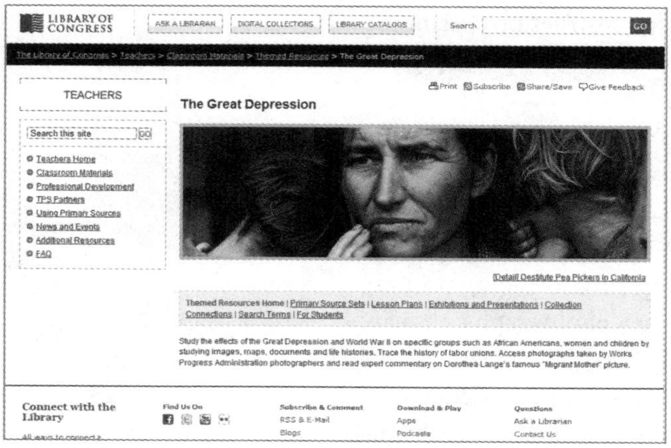

**FIGURE 2.2**
Screen capture of the "Themed Resources: The Great Depression" from the "Teachers" page of the Library of Congress website.

## HIGHLIGHTS OF "THEMED RESOURCES"

- Browse topics to find related classroom materials. Each themed resource includes links to other classroom materials on the same topic. These resources include "Primary Source Sets," "Lesson Plans," "Exhibitions and Presentations," and "Collection Connections."
- Search the library's digital collections for items related to the theme. A list of related search terms is provided for each themed resource. When searching for primary source materials, it is important to consider the historic name given to an event or object. The lists of search terms are useful for finding historic names or synonyms. For example, under the theme "Advertising," recommended search terms include *billboards, broadsides, emblems,* and *logos.*
- Find Library of Congress resources written for students. The "For Students" section links to appropriate interactive online presentations related to each themed resource that can be assigned as homework, as extension activities for individual students, or integrated into lessons using classroom technology.

## "PRIMARY SOURCE SETS"

The "Primary Source Sets" section is collections of fifteen to twenty primary sources on topics ranging from children's lives at the turn of the twentieth century (fig. 2.3) to the Harlem Renaissance. Each set includes a variety of primary source formats such as manuscripts, photographs, sheet music, maps, and sound recordings. "Primary Source Sets" provides a list of suggestions for using the primary sources in the classroom. The flexible formats allow K–12 teachers to choose the most engaging and accessible primary sources and integrate them into their classroom teaching. For example, a photograph in the "Women's Suffrage" set (fig. 2.4) is accessible to elementary students, while high school students can interpret the political cartoons included in the same set.

FIGURE 2.3
Screen capture of "Children's Lives at the Turn of the Twentieth Century" from the Library of Congress "Primary Source Sets Teacher's Guide."

## HIGHLIGHTS OF "PRIMARY SOURCE SETS"

- **Printable teacher's guide.** The guide may be downloaded as a PDF file and includes all primary source set materials.
- **Background historical information.** Teachers can refresh their background knowledge of a historical topic or use the historical background to launch additional research into a new topic.
- **Multilevel activities.** To get you started, the Educational Outreach team has included a list of suggestions for teachers. The set provides three to five classroom activities for using the primary sources in the classroom. These suggestions are easily adaptable to different grade levels and can spur other ideas for using the primary sources in classroom instruction.
- **Additional resources.** Links provide access to related collections available on the Library of Congress website.
- **Citation information.** Will you be using the primary source in a presentation? The citation of each primary source in the set is included in the teacher's guide.
- **Multiple links to primary sources.**
  - Thumbnail images link to where the primary source lives on the Library of Congress website.
  - Titles link to the bibliographic record for the item. The bibliographic record gives students additional information about each primary source.
  - Full-page, high-quality PDFs can be downloaded for each primary source. The links provide a full-page version that can be printed or projected for students to analyze. Maps are split into four pages to better facilitate a map analysis activity and to ensure that it is large enough to see all the details.

**FIGURE 2.4**
Screen capture of the "Primary Source Sets: Women's Suffrage" from the "Teachers" page of the Library of Congress website.

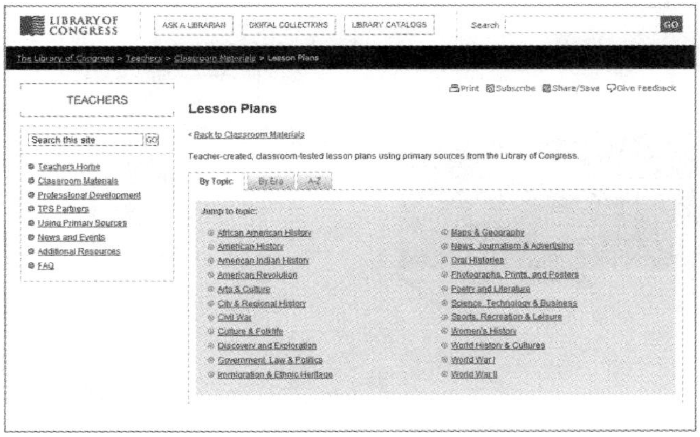

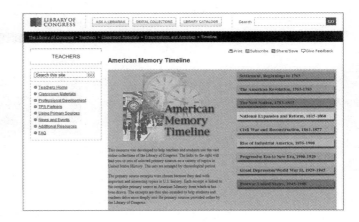

**FIGURE 2.5**
Screen capture of "Lesson Plans" by topic from the "Teachers" page on the Library of Congress website.

**FIGURE 2.6**
Screen capture of *American Memory* Timeline," from the "Teachers" page under "Classroom Materials/Presentations" on the Library of Congress website.

## "LESSON PLANS"

In 1997, the Library of Congress initiated the American Memory Fellows Program, bringing twenty-five pairs of K–12 teachers and school librarians to the library to explore the collections and create lesson plans and other teaching activities.[2] The Library of Congress American Memory Fellows developed and tested most of the lesson plans featured on the "Teachers" page.

Lesson plans are organized in the "Classroom Materials" section under three tabs—by topic, era, and title (fig. 2.5)—along with the suggested grade level. Many of the lesson plans were created by middle- and high-school teachers and can be used as written or adapted for use at other grade levels.

### HIGHLIGHTS OF "LESSON PLANS"

- The overview page provides a brief description of the lesson and includes learning objectives and an estimated time for completion.
- The "Preparation" section lists all of the necessary materials and provides links to PDFs.
- Step-by-step directions help teachers implement the lesson and extension activities.

## "PRESENTATIONS & ACTIVITIES"

Presentations investigate curricular themes and put primary sources from the Library of Congress *American Memory* collections into context. Each presentation visually represents primary sources and background information differently, for example, some themes are represented chronologically on a timeline (fig. 2.6) and others geographically on a map. Activities are designed to allow students to interact with the content. Most presentations and activities are accessible by students, but depending on the grade level it may be necessary to have teacher guidance.

FIGURE 2.7
Screen capture of
"African American Odyssey,"
a "Collections Connections"
feature of the "Teachers" page.

## HIGHLIGHTS OF "PRESENTATIONS & ACTIVITIES"

- *"American Memory* **timeline."** Primary sources that cover important and interesting topics in US history are arranged in chronological order.
- **"Immigration."** Immigration in the United States is explored using primary sources that focus on the largest immigrant groups from the nineteenth and early twentieth centuries.
- **"Lyrical Legacy."** Eighteen American songs and poems are represented by an original primary source document, historical background, and, in many cases, sound recordings.
- **"Taking the Mystery out of Copyright."** Students explore copyright as it relates to their lives.

## "COLLECTION CONNECTIONS"

"Collection Connections" provides brief summaries and teaching resources for most of the Library of Congress collections (fig. 2.7). Many of the manuscript, photograph, and other *American Memory* collections are listed in alphabetical order on the "Teachers" Page.

## HIGHLIGHTS OF "COLLECTION CONNECTIONS"

- Each "Collection Connection" has a summary page that provides an overview of the collection and the historical eras it encompasses, as well as links to related collections and exhibits.
- Collections with teaching resources provide historical context for the collection and activities for using the primary sources to build critical thinking skills and integrating the primary sources into the arts and humanities.

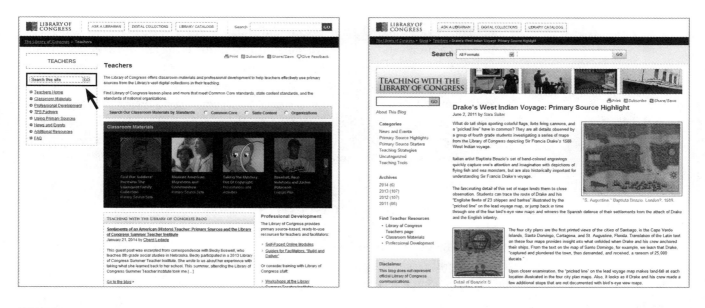

**FIGURE 2.8**
Screen capture of the Library of Congress "Teachers" page showing the keyword search box.

**FIGURE 2.9**
Screen capture of the "Drake's West Indian Voyage: Primary Source Highlight" post from the blog *Teaching with the Library of Congress*.

## QUICK SEARCH TIPS FOR THE "TEACHERS" PAGE

Classroom materials on the "Teachers" page are well organized by theme and topic and encourage discovery by browsing. The Educational Outreach team understands that when it's crunch time, it can be difficult to find the time to browse. The "Teachers" page has built-in search functions that enable teachers to quickly see what materials are available.

The new search-by-standards feature lets teachers search classroom materials by Common Core State Standards, state, grade level, and subject—current choices include social studies, language arts, and library/technology. When using this search feature, it is important to remember that many of the classroom materials can be adapted for use at a range of grade levels. Limiting your search to a particular grade level, especially the lower elementary grades, might not turn up many results, but that doesn't mean there isn't anything relevant to your topic on the site. The search-by-standards feature is a good way to quickly discover if there are any resources related to a particular standard, but it shouldn't be the only place you check.

Searching keywords in the "Search this Site" box (fig. 2.8) will return all classroom materials on the "Teachers" page that correspond with your search. This is another way to quickly see what classroom materials are available, but the list may not be exhaustive depending on the keywords you search. Under each link is a description of the type of resource (e.g. "Themed Resources," "Primary Source Sets," or "Collection Connections").

## THE *TEACHING WITH THE LIBRARY OF CONGRESS* BLOG

The *Teaching with the Library of Congress* blog (fig. 2.9) provides a forum for discovery of primary sources and discussion of strategies for using primary sources in the classroom. The Educational Outreach team and subject-matter experts regularly highlight primary collections and provide teaching strategies for using these resources to build critical thinking skills, engage students, and construct knowledge. Blog postings place the primary source in historical context and provide background on items highlighted from the collection. Posts are organized into categories depending on their content focus. The categories include: Primary Source Highlights, Primary Source Starters, Teaching Strategies, and Teaching Tools. The blog encourages practicing teachers and school librarians to share ideas and examples from their own practice.

## "PRIMARY SOURCE HIGHLIGHTS"

"Primary Source Highlights" posts focus on a single primary source or collection available on the library's website. Each post contains three to five teaching ideas for using the primary source in the classroom as well as links to additional resources from the Library of Congress. "Primary Source Highlights" gives Educational Outreach staff a chance to highlight unique items, often corresponding with holidays or current events. See "Theodore Roosevelt's Thanksgiving Truce" for a sample post with a new twist for Thanksgiving (fig. 2.10).

FIGURE 2.10
Reproduction of the "Theodore Roosevelt's Thanksgiving Truce: Primary Source Highlight" blog post.

PUCK

A THANKSGIVING TRUCE.

THE BEAR (with deep feeling).—Here's hoping that when next we meet, we see you first.

## THEODORE ROOSEVELT'S THANKSGIVING TRUCE: A POLITICAL CARTOON

*November 10th, 2011, by Stacie Moats*

The familiar imagery of Thanksgiving has been put to many different uses over the years. Let your students explore how one cartoonist used the holiday to make points about President Theodore Roosevelt. Some of your students may only know TR as one of the characters in a popular movie about a museum that comes to life at night. Consider using this cartoon to introduce students to some key facts about this larger-than-life figure in American history and the times in which he lived.

Observing the details of the cartoon can provide students with more than just a few laughs; upon closer examination, it offers clues about Roosevelt's life and passions. For instance, Roosevelt is depicted wearing his Rough Rider uniform, according to the item record. Students can use other Library of Congress resources to learn more about the story of Roosevelt and his Rough Riders, the first volunteer cavalry unit in the Spanish-American War.

Students of all ages may be able to personally relate to the cartoon's depiction of a kids' table set up beside the grown-ups' table at Thanksgiving. The table's two occupants, Teddy Jr. and a bear cub, each may lead students to dig deeper into the Library's digitized collections for evidence of Theodore Roosevelt's personal history. For example, students may read handwritten letters with drawings that Roosevelt sent to his young son, Teddy Jr., which indicates a loving father-son relationship. Or perhaps students may observe a cartoon by Clifford Berryman of Roosevelt with a teddy bear cub and seek evidence about the legendary incident that inspired its creation as well as countless "Teddy bears" for generations of children.

The cartoon's title and theme of "A Thanksgiving Truce" itself draws attention to Roosevelt's deep and complex relationship with nature. Both an avid hunter and animal lover, Roosevelt arguably made his most lasting contributions as a conservationist. At the time of this cartoon's publication, Roosevelt was about halfway through a White House tenure that resulted in the designation of National Forests, National Parks, National Game Preserves, and more.

**After analyzing this cartoon, students can:**

- Re-envision this cartoon's theme, "A Thanksgiving Truce," from a modern perspective. Describe a group of individuals in American politics or news today unlikely to celebrate this national holiday together. What toast might they make during their truce and why?
- Create a timeline of Roosevelt's life. Draw a cartoon depicting another aspect of Roosevelt's public service or personal character.
- Create a hypothetical narrative of the legacy of Roosevelt's contributions as a conservationist from a wild animal's point of view or from a hunter's point of view.

To learn more about Theodore Roosevelt's life and times, check out his entry and more in the *Meet Amazing Americans* section of America's Library.

Or, investigate the *Theodore Roosevelt Papers*, one of the Library's largest Presidential collections.

How else might you use this or another political cartoon to introduce students to an important figure or event from American history?

*Posted in: Primary Source Highlights*

Source: Stacie Moats, "Theodore Roosevelt's Thanksgiving Truce: A Political Cartoon," *Teaching with the Library of Congress* (blog), November 10, 2011, http://blogs.loc.gov/teachers/2011/11/theodore-roosevelts-thanksgiving-truce-a-political-cartoon.

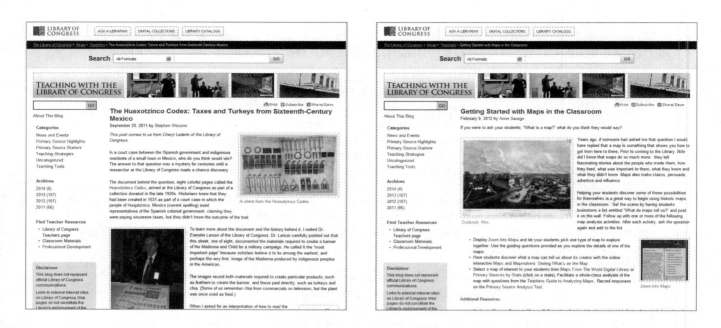

**FIGURE 2.11**
Screen capture of "The Huexotzinco Codex: Taxes and Turkeys from Sixteenth-Century Mexico," a "Primary Source Starters" blog post by Stephen Wesson.

**FIGURE 2.12**
Screen capture of "Getting Started with Maps in the Classroom," a "Teaching Strategies" blog post by Anne Savage.

## "PRIMARY SOURCE STARTERS"

"Primary Source Starters" posts (fig. 2.11) feature one primary source and related teaching ideas for immediate classroom use. The goal of these posts is for teachers or school librarians to have a ready-to-use primary source analysis activity that can be printed or projected and used to build critical thinking skills.

## "TEACHING STRATEGIES"

The mission of the Educational Outreach Division is to support teachers' use of primary sources to build critical thinking and analysis skills. The "Teaching Strategies" posts focus on how to use primary sources in the classroom. Topics covered include effective questioning techniques; how to use certain formats, such as maps (fig. 2.12), in the classroom; and strategies for building observation skills in young learners. These posts discuss pedagogy for facilitating successful primary source analysis activities.

## QUICK SEARCH TIPS FOR THE
## *TEACHING WITH THE LIBRARY OF CONGRESS* BLOG

To conduct a quick scan of the topics covered in the blog posts, plug a keyword into the "Search this Blog" box. The full-text search will return every instance the keyword is mentioned in the *Teaching with the Library of Congress* blog.

## GETTING STARTED:
## TOOLS FOR TEACHING WITH PRIMARY SOURCES

With thousands of digitized primary sources from which to choose, it is important to consider several factors in order to select the most engaging and effective primary source. Factors include choosing items that are accessible to students, considering the historical context and perspective of the primary source, and selecting a high-quality primary source that lends itself to close analysis. After a primary source is selected, a visit to the "Teachers" page will provide the tools and teaching ideas for integrating the primary source into instruction.

## SELECTING ACCESSIBLE PRIMARY SOURCES

Primary sources that engage but are also accessible to students will ensure a positive impact on student learning (fig. 2.13). The following are considerations for selecting accessible primary sources:

- **Content.** Will your students want to look closely, ask questions, and learn more about this particular primary source?
- **Age-appropriateness.** Is the content suitable for your students? Is it too complex?
- **Length.** Will the length of the letter, diary entry, or newspaper article affect student comprehension? Is an excerpt more appropriate?
- **Readability of text or handwriting.** Is text clearly printed and legible? Will cursive handwriting affect your students' understanding?
- **Reading level of students.** Will your students be able to decode the text of the primary source?
- **Prior knowledge needed (historical, vocabulary).** Do outdated terms need to be defined? Will your students understand the content of the primary source?[3]

FIGURE 2.13
*The Mealing Trough—Hopi, c1906.*
Photograph by Edward S. Curtis.
Library of Congress Prints and
Photographs Division.

## CONSIDERING HISTORICAL CONTEXT

When students think like historians, they go beyond memorizing names and dates and construct their own understanding of historical events by piecing together evidence from multiple sources—both primary and secondary. It is important for teachers to select primary sources with enough information for students to place the photograph, diary entry, or map within historical context (fig. 2.14).

Understanding the historical context of a primary source is critical for understanding the attitudes and influences that shaped the source's creation; otherwise, a primary source's true meaning might be misinterpreted. Here are some characteristics to look for when selecting primary sources that your students will be able to place within historical context:

- **Bibliographic information.** How detailed is the item's bibliographic record? Do your students need a primary source with a more descriptive bibliographic record so they can find more leads for their research project?
- **Creator name and creation/publication date.** Are the creator's name and creation date available on the primary source or in the bibliographic record? Are you studying point of view and therefore need to identify the creator of a particular primary source?
- **Time and topic under study in your classroom.** What is the time and topic under study in your classroom? Is the source considered a primary source (created at the time under study) or a secondary source (accounts or interpretations of events created by someone without firsthand experience)?
- **Contextual clues.** Are there clues within the primary source that will help students place the primary source in context? Will students identify clothing or technology from a certain time period?
- **Extraneous markings or annotations.** Will Library of Congress cataloguer's notes or other markings distract your students and interfere with their ability to place the primary source within historical context?[4]

FIGURE 2.14
*Oakland, Calif., Feb. 1942.*
Photograph by Dorothea Lange.
Library of Congress Prints and
Photographs Division.

FIGURE 2.15
*Part of the Vast Billboard Campaign of the Woman's Party. Putting Up Billboard in Denver—1916.* Library of Congress Manuscript Division.

## THINKING ABOUT PERSPECTIVE

Primary sources present students with multiple perspectives and teach them to ask questions and think critically (fig. 2.15). When students analyze primary sources, they might encounter a new idea that challenges their beliefs. They must weigh evidence from multiple sources and find information to explain incongruities. Once students have the skills to recognize that there is a point of view present in every textbook, news program, or advertisement, they will be more likely to seek out the other side—or sides—of any story. When selecting primary sources, consider several factors that might help your students identify point of view:

- **Creator.** Will your students be able to find out who created the primary source? How much information can they find out about the creator's beliefs or other works?
- **Target audience and purpose of the primary source.** Can students infer the intended audience for the primary source, and whether the creator might have been promoting a certain idea or agenda?
- **Circumstances of creation.** Will students be familiar with any of the personal, social, cultural, or political events that surrounded the creation of the primary source?
- **Your own point of view.** Consider your own beliefs about a historical event or issue. By selecting a particular primary source, are you inadvertently presenting one point of view over another?
- **Different perspectives.** When using more than one primary source, have you selected items that present different perspectives?
- **Overall meaning preserved.** If you plan to use an excerpt of a primary source, is the meaning of the entire primary source preserved?[5]

## CONSIDER QUALITY

Whether printing or projecting a primary source, it is important that students are able to see details to support their analysis (fig. 2.16). When selecting high-quality primary sources to use with your students, consider the following factors:

- **Clarity, resolution.** Are you using the highest quality image or film available on the library's website? Is the image or film clear enough for students to find important details and make reflections about what's happening?
  *Note: Images on the Library of Congress website often have several downloadable versions, including various JPEG and TIFF file sizes. Consider using a larger file type when projecting an image or enlarging an image for printable handouts.*
- **Legibility of the text or handwriting.** Is the text clearly printed and legible? Can your students read and understand cursive handwriting?
  *Note: Transcripts accompany some digitized manuscripts from the library's collections. Although the transcripts are generally considered secondary sources, they are a tool that can accompany a primary source and make it easier to use with students.*
- **Audibility, background noises.** Is the voice in the sound recording or film loud and clear enough for students to understand the message? Are there background noises that make the message inaudible?
  *Note: The Library of Congress's "National Jukebox" includes more than ten thousand recordings made by the Victor Talking Machine Company between 1901 and 1925. You can browse the recordings and create playlists to stream in class.*
- **Ability to zoom in on details.** Do the digitized images or maps have the ability to zoom in on details? Can the same zoom ability be recreated in print form, or is the primary source best used in its digital format?
  *Note: The digitized maps from the library's map collections have a zoom view that enables viewers to find minute details on the high-resolution maps.*[6]

FIGURE 2.16
*View of Washington City.*
Lithograph and print by
E. Sachse & Co.
Library of Congress Prints
and Photographs Division.

VIEW OF WASHINGTON CITY.

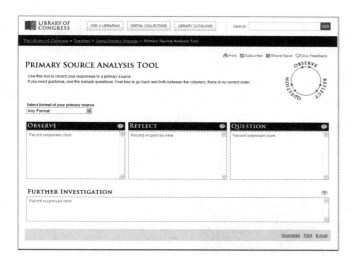

FIGURE 2.17
Reproduction of the "Primary Source Analysis Tool" from the
"Using Primary Sources" section of the "Teachers" page of the
Library of Congress website.

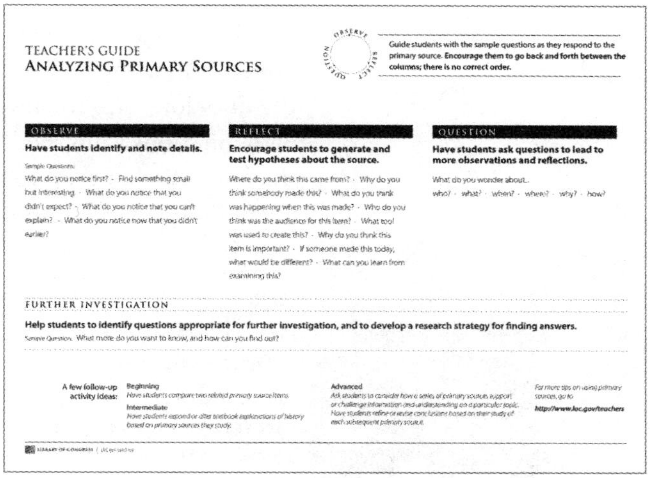

FIGURE 2.18
Reproduction of "Teacher's Guide: Analyzing Primary Sources"
from the "Using Primary Sources" section of the "Teachers" page
of the Library of Congress website.

## THE PRIMARY SOURCE ANALYSIS TOOL
## AND TEACHER'S GUIDES

The Educational Outreach team developed the Primary Source Analysis Tool (fig. 2.17)
to guide students' analysis of primary sources. The analysis process is not linear and involves moving back and forth between the three columns—observe, reflect, and question.
Making observations often brings questions to mind, and it is okay to record those in
the question column. Students record details they notice in the observe column of the
Primary Source Analysis Tool. When students share their observations, they can pinpoint
their observations by saying, "*I see* five people" or "*I hear* something that sounds like a
ringing bell."

The reflect column is used to record inferences or hypotheses drawn from observed
details. It is important to recognize where our reflections come from. Are they based on
details we noticed through observation or from our prior knowledge? When students
share reflections, encourage them to identify the origin of their reflection: "*I think* there's
a battle *because I noticed* the cannons with smoke and fire."

Finally, the question column appears to be the most straightforward column, but is
also the most important. The questions recorded in this column will be the starting point
for further investigation. Students can share their questions, such as "*I wonder*, why isn't
the boy wearing shoes?"

The "Teachers" page includes teacher's guides to help facilitate the primary source
analysis process. Each teacher's guide includes questions for each column of the Primary
Source Analysis Tool (fig. 2.18). These questions are used to guide students through the
analysis process. The questions were developed in concert with subject matter experts.
When the experts receive a new item in their collections, they ask themselves these same
questions in order to think critically about the primary sources.

Teachers use the questions in different ways. It's best to select a few questions from each column. You may decide to highlight these questions on the teacher's guide, or type the questions into the fillable PDF to guide students. Approaching each primary source with questions from the Primary Source Analysis Tool will help students become critical thinkers whether they are questioning a historical document or a current website.

Still looking for more? Venture out to the Library of Congress website.

**American Memory**
**http://memory.loc.gov**

American Memory provides access to primary source materials that document the American experience. American Memory collections can be browsed by topic, time period, format, and place.[7]

**Prints and Photographs**
**Online Catalog**
**www.loc.gov/pictures**

The Prints and Photographs Online Catalog (PPOC) features digital images that can be browsed by collection or searched with the search box on the homepage. PPOC offers a range of viewing options, including a slide show function. Items are available as downloadable JPEGs or TIFFs.[8]

**Chronicling America:**
**Historic American Newspapers**
**http://chroniclingamerica.loc.gov**

Chronicling America provides access to select historic American newspaper pages from 1836–1922. Newspapers can be searched by state or title, and results further narrowed by date range, ethnicity, and language. With searchable full text, keywords are highlighted on each page. Also includes recommended topics.[9]

**World Digital Library**
**www.wdl.org**

The World Digital Library partners with libraries, archives, and other national cultural institutions to provide access to digitized cultural treasures from around the world. WDL provides access to a range of primary sources including photographs, maps, and multivolume books. The site is available in seven languages, and items can be browsed by place, time, topic, type of item, and contributing institution.[10]

**Veterans History Project**
**www.loc.gov/vets**

The Veterans History Project (VHP) collects oral histories from American war veterans. In addition to audio and video recordings, VHP accepts, preserves, and makes available online collections of photographs, letters, and other historical documents. Volunteers can participate in the project by conducting interviews with veterans.[11]

**National Jukebox**
**www.loc.gov/jukebox**

The National Jukebox features thousands of historical sound recordings made between 1901 and 1925 by the Victor Talking Machine Company. Users can stream the recordings for free, browse by genre or artist, and create and save playlists for future access.[12]

## NOTES

1. Sara Suiter, "Teacher Resources at the Library of Congress," *Medium, Journal of the Washington Library Media Association* 35, no. 2 (2011): 16–17, http://issuu.com/wlma-medium -journal/docs/wlma_medium_winter2011v35n2.

2. "National Digital Library Program," Library of Congress, accessed March 5, 2012, http://memory.loc.gov/ammem/dli2/html/lcndlp.html.

3. Sara Suiter, "Selecting Primary Sources, Part I: Knowing your Students," *Teaching with the Library of Congress* (blog), July 12, 2011, http://blogs.loc.gov/teachers/2011/07/selecting -primary-sources-part-i-knowing-your-students.

4. Sara Suiter, "Selecting Primary Sources, Part II: Considering Historical Context," *Teaching with the Library of Congress* (blog), July 26, 2011, http://blogs.loc.gov/teachers/2011/07/ selecting-primary-sources-part-ii-considering-historical-context.

5. Sara Suiter, "Selecting Primary Sources, Part III: Thinking about Perspective," *Teaching with the Library of Congress* (blog), August 9, 2011, http://blogs.loc.gov/teachers/2011/08/selecting -primary-sources-part-iii-thinking-about-perspective.

6. Sara Suiter, "Selecting Primary Sources, Part IV: Considering Quality," *Teaching with the Library of Congress* (blog), August 25, 2011, http://blogs.loc.gov/teachers/2011/08/selecting -primary-sources-part-iv-considering-quality .

7. *[Front Cover of Jackie Robinson Comic Book]*, digital image, 1951, Library of Congress, accessed September 20, 2012, www.loc.gov/pictures/item/97519504.

8. Dorothea Lange, *Migrant Mother; Destitute Pea Pickers in California*, digital image, 1936, Library of Congress Prints and Photographs Division, www.loc.gov/pictures/item/ fsa1998021539/PP.

9. *The Tacoma Times. Image 1. (Tacoma, Wash.) 1903–1949*, Library of Congress, May 18, 1910, http://chroniclingamerica.loc.gov/lccn/sn88085187/1910-05-18/ed-1/seq-1.

10. *World Digital Library Logo*, digital image, World Digital Library Home, accessed September 20, 2012, www.wdl.org/en.

11. *[World War I Soldier with American Flag in Background]*, digital image, 1914, Library of Congress Prints and Photographs Division, www.loc.gov/pictures/item/2010651602.

12. John Vachon, *Farmer Examining Phonograph. Auction near Tenstrike, Minnesota*, digital image, September 1939, Library of Congress Prints and Photographs Division, www.loc.gov/ pictures/item/fsa1997004572/PP.

## BIBLIOGRAPHY

"African American Odyssey." Library of Congress. www.loc.gov/teachers/classroommaterials/ connections/afam-odyssey.

"American History Timeline." Library of Congress. www.loc.gov/teachers/classroommaterials/ presentationsandactivities/presentations/timeline.

Curtis, Edward S. *The Mealing Trough—Hopi c1906*. Digital image. Library of Congress Prints and Photographs Division. www.loc.gov/pictures/item/92519541.

"The Great Depression." Library of Congress. www.loc.gov/teachers/classroommaterials/themes/ great-depression.

Lange, Dorothea. *Oakland, Calif., Feb. 1942*. Digital image. Library of Congress Prints and Photographs Division. www.loc.gov/pictures/item/2001705924.

"Lesson Plans." Library of Congress. www.loc.gov/teachers/classroommaterials/lessons.

Library of Congress Educational Outreach Division. *Children's Lives at the Turn of the Twentieth Century*. Teacher's guide. www.loc.gov/teachers/classroommaterials/primarysourcesets/childrens-lives/pdf/teacher_guide.pdf.

Moats, Stacie. "Theodore Roosevelt's Thanksgiving Truce: A Political Cartoon." *Teaching with the Library of Congress* (blog), November 10, 2011. http://blogs.loc.gov/teachers/2011/11/theodore-roosevelts-thanksgiving-truce-a-political-cartoon.

"National Digital Library Program." Library of Congress. http://memory.loc.gov/ammem/dli2/html/lcndlp.html.

*Part of the Vast Billboard Campaign of the Woman's Party. Putting up Billboard in Denver—1916.* Digital image. Library of Congress Manuscript Division. http://hdl.loc.gov/loc.mss/mnwp.159016.

"Primary Source Analysis Tool." Library of Congress. www.loc.gov/teachers/usingprimarysources/resources/Primary_Source_Analysis_Tool.pdf.

Pughe, John S. *A Thanksgiving Truce*. Digital image. Library of Congress Prints and Photographs Division. www.loc.gov/pictures/item/2011645756.

Sachse & Co, E. *View of Washington City, Lithograph and Print*. Digital image. Library of Congress Prints and Photographs Division. www.loc.gov/pictures/item/00650779.

Savage, Anne. "Getting Started with Maps in the Classroom." *Teaching with the Library of Congress* (blog), February 9, 2012. http://blogs.loc.gov/teachers/2012/02/getting-started-with-maps-in-the-classroom.

Suiter, Sara. "Drake's West Indian Voyage: Primary Source Highlight." *Teaching with the Library of Congress* (blog), June 2, 2011. http://blogs.loc.gov/teachers/2011/06/drake%E2%80%99s-west-indian-voyage-primary-source-highlight.

———. "Teacher Resources at the Library of Congress." *Medium, Journal of the Washington Library Media Association* 35, no. 2 (2011): 16–17. http://issuu.com/wlma-medium-journal/docs/wlma_medium_winter2011v35n2.

"Teacher's Guide: Analyzing Primary Sources." Library of Congress. www.loc.gov/teachers/usingprimarysources/resources/Analyzing_Primary_Sources.pdf.

"Teacher's Guides and Analysis Tool." Library of Congress. www.loc.gov/teachers/usingprimarysources/guides.html.

"Teachers." Library of Congress. www.loc.gov/teachers.

Wesson, Stephen. "The Huexotzinco Codex: Taxes and Turkeys from Sixteenth-Century Mexico." *Teaching with the Library of Congress* (blog), September 20, 2011. http://blogs.loc.gov/teachers/2011/09/the-huexotzinco-codex-taxes-and-turkeys-from-sixteenth-century-mexico.

"Women's Suffrage Primary Source Set." Library of Congress. www.loc.gov/teachers/classroommaterials/primarysourcesets/womens-suffrage.

# Professional Development and Support for Classroom Teachers Available through the Library of Congress

KATHARINE LEHMAN

Look at these artifacts: a pocket watch, a Confederate five-dollar bill, a pair of old glasses, and several old newspaper clippings placed on a table. If you were told they came out of the pocket of a gentleman who lived in the mid-1860s, what kind of profile would you make of him?

How old might he be? What part of the country does he live in? Is he rich, poor, middle class? How educated would he be? Think about this a minute before reading on.

The truth is that similar artifacts were found in Abraham Lincoln's pockets the night he was assassinated (fig. 3.1). Are you surprised by any of them? Would you or your students be curious why he carried a Confederate bill? Primary sources spark our curiosity to learn more and investigate circumstances surrounding an event more closely. Where had Lincoln been in the days before he went to Ford's Theater?

Now look at the headlines from some of the newspaper clippings he had tucked in his wallet: "Emancipation in Missouri," "Message of the Governor of Missouri," "Disaffection among Southern Soldiers," "Conscript's Epistle to Jeff Davis," "Sherman's Orders

FIGURE 3.1
Artifact samples for staff in-service on *Lincoln's Pockets*. Photograph by Katharine Lehman.

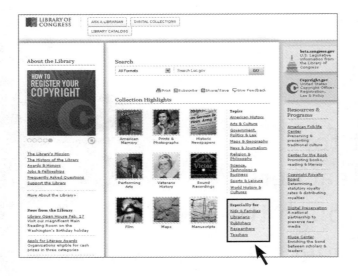

FIGURE 3.2
Screen capture of the
Library of Congress home page.

for his March," "The Two Platforms: Lincoln and Johnson; McClellan and Pendleton." Based on these headlines, what do you think was on Lincoln's mind the night he went to the theater? You might leave this introductory lesson with more questions about Abraham Lincoln than answers. How many new research paths have been opened? What do these articles tell us about the man?

*Lincoln's Pockets* is one of the introductory modules in the TPS Direct Professional Development Builder program available online from the "Teachers" page on the Library of Congress website. For those who cannot attend a Summer Teacher Institute at the library in person, or wish to return to their home districts from a Library of Congress workshop and lead a professional development workshop similar to the one they experienced in Washington, DC, high-quality staff development is freely available from the "Teachers" page.

The exercise described at the beginning of this chapter was the introductory set conducted with a group of librarians in Chesterfield County, Virginia, for an in-service day workshop. In this historic community (which still maintains sites and markers of Civil War battles waged in the defense of Richmond), no one guessed similar artifacts were discovered in the pockets of a union sympathizer, much less the president of the United States. To see pictures of the actual artifacts found in Lincoln's pockets and to access materials to develop your own staff development workshop, begin at the Library of Congress home page and click on "Teachers" (fig. 3.2).

Under "Professional Development," teachers and facilitators have several options. Self-paced modules link to online videos providing panoramic tours and explanations of the library. There are overviews of collections with guides to evaluate and analyze primary source items. The "Build and Deliver" professional development modules empower presenters to customize staff development workshops in home school districts. For those who can come to Washington, there are opportunities at the Library of Congress for workshops, as well as the weeklong Summer Teacher Institute. For those who cannot come to Washington, videoconferencing is available with Library of Congress staff. Regionally across the United States there are participating TPS (Teaching with Primary Sources) partners offering programs and training for schools. All these opportunities to connect students with primary sources are no more than two clicks away from the Library of Congress home page.

## SETTING UP YOUR OWN STAFF DEVELOPMENT

On the "Teachers" page, select "Professional Development" from the menu. The Professional Development modules are divided into two sections: "Build and Deliver" and "Take Online Modules" (fig. 3.3).

## "TAKE ONLINE MODULES"

The online modules (fig. 3.4) offer teachers and staff development presenters an introduction to the Library of Congress, its collections, and best practices for using primary sources in the classroom. Each module is a multimedia feast—and each one guides the viewer through examples of artifacts available in the collection as well as instruction in copyright and ethical use of the resources. The modules are approximately one hour long and offer certificates of completion at the end. The ultimate goal of these modules is to instruct teachers in the richness of using primary sources to engage students and spark their interest in questioning and further research.

As an overview of the library and its collections, the modules introduce inquiry learning as an approach for teaching with primary sources. Staff development leaders who have not been to the library for instruction will want to begin with these overview modules before using the "Build and Deliver" modules. Topics include understanding copyright, analyzing prints and photographs, analyzing maps, and finding primary sources. Teachers attending the in-house workshops and Summer Institutes are asked to view the introduction to the Library of Congress and the copyright modules before coming to the library. All the modules are free and can be viewed individually or in groups for faculty in-services.

Additional modules are being planned, so expect this resource to grow in value over time. Primary sources are a natural springboard to high-level critical thinking and learning, as shown in the lessons and resources in this chapter and others. Links to analysis tools and strategies for classroom use are found in the "Teachers" page menu under the links "Using Primary Sources" and "Classroom Materials."

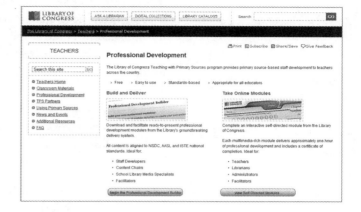

FIGURE 3.3
Screen capture of the Library of Congress "Professional Development" overview web page.

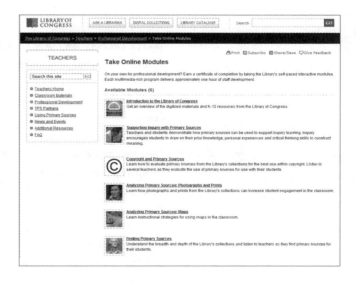

FIGURE 3.4
Screen capture of the Library of Congress "Take Online Modules" web page.

## "BUILD AND DELIVER"

This chapter begins with a sample introductory set from "Build and Deliver" that can be used in a staff development session to hook the audience. The session description can be downloaded in HTML and PDF formats with an overview of how primary documents create a window into our present lives and the past. Goals, objectives, materials, procedures, and assessment suggestions are provided. Standards for the lessons have been aligned with AASL's *Standards for the 21st-Century Learner*, ISTE's (International Society for Technology in Education's) technology standards for students and teachers, and NSDC (National Society for Staff Development) standards.[1]

In addition to studying the evidence Lincoln left, teachers will encourage students to look in their own pockets and backpacks.

- What evidence do students carry that reveal facts about them, what they think about, and what their interests are?
- What activities during the past twenty-four hours will leave evidence of their existence? Receipts? Ticket stubs? Homework? E-mail? Text messages? Voice mail?
- Which of these will leave a trace?
- Which are primary sources?
- If someone returned from the future, what could they tell about you from what you leave behind?

This is the complementary lesson to *Lincoln's Pockets*, titled "Leaving Evidence of Our Lives." Once the two introductory lessons are complete and an understanding of primary sources is mastered, it is time to begin analyzing documents and artifacts in the remaining modules.

## BUILDING YOUR CUSTOMIZED PROFESSIONAL DEVELOPMENT PROGRAM

In "Build and Deliver," use the check boxes to select the content modules you wish to cover for the time you have available (fig. 3.5). The amount of time recommended to complete each module is estimated in the box to the right. The number of activities and required time will change in the "Activities You've Selected" box as you add or detract modules. Once the staff development sessions are checked, click "Continue" for final selection of your materials. There is no charge; however, the Library of Congress asks for your zip code to track where requests are originating. Additional modules are listed in figure 3.6 and include in-depth strategies for connecting with primary sources, analyzing music as historical artifacts, increasing perception through photography, matching literature and primary sources through book backdrops, and delving into specific topics, such as "Exploring American Treasures" and "Understanding Copyright." Specific modules focus on understanding the inquiry process and creating inquiry activities with primary sources.

## USING THE MODULES FOR STAFF DEVELOPMENT

### THE TPS DIRECT GUIDE INSTRUCTS TEACHERS

Teaching with primary sources can facilitate:

1. Student engagement

   - Primary sources help students relate in a personal way to events of the past and promote a deeper understanding of cultural history as a series of human events.
   - Because primary sources are snippets of the past, they encourage students to seek additional evidence through research.
   - First-person accounts of events help make them more real, fostering active reading and response.

2. Development of critical thinking skills

   - Many state standards support teaching with primary sources, which require students to be both critical and analytical as they read and examine documents and objects.
   - Primary sources are often incomplete and have little context. Students must use prior knowledge and work with multiple primary sources to find patterns.
   - In analyzing primary sources, students move from concrete observations and facts to questioning and making inferences about the materials.
   - Questions of creator bias, purpose, and point of view may challenge students' assumptions.

3. Construction of knowledge

   - Inquiry into primary sources encourages students to wrestle with contradictions and compare multiple sources that represent differing points of view, confronting the complexity of the past.
   - Students construct knowledge as they form reasoned conclusions, base their conclusions on evidence, and connect primary sources to the context in which they were created, synthesizing information from multiple sources.

Source: Library of Congress, *TPS Direct: Teaching with Primary Sources*, PDF, December 9, 2010, iii.

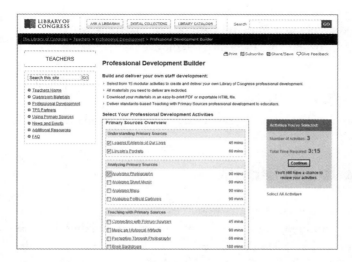

FIGURE 3.5
Screen capture of the Library of Congress "Professional Development Builder" modules.

FIGURE 3.6
Screen capture of the Library of Congress "Professional Development Builder" modules.

FIGURE 3.7
*Dotheboys Hall in Session.
Huntsville, Alabama. 1913.*
Photograph by
Lewis Wicker Hine.
Library of Congress Prints
and Photographs Division.

When analyzing photographs, for example, participants in the staff development session will focus on examples from the National Child Labor Committee (US) Library of Congress Prints and Photographs Division. These prints depict haunting examples of children at work and in schools (fig. 3.7). Participants will practice looking carefully and recording what they see on the "Photograph Analysis" sheet provided (see also fig. 2.17). They will wonder about what is happening beyond the picture. They will use prior knowledge to put the photographs in historical context and develop questions for further study.

Teachers in the workshop must grapple with the complexities of studying primary source documents—the same complexities that their students will face. From this experience, participants will be better able to help students construct new knowledge based on what they learn from the photographs and times they study. Primary sources are the raw materials of history, created by the people who lived through the event or issue represented. These sources can be complex and sometimes contradictory. Students new to using primary sources need guidance from teachers to develop the higher-level critical thinking skills needed to understand and analyze them. Presented in engaging lessons, primary sources invite open-ended questions and inspire inquiring minds to research and read more.

## BOOK BACKDROPS AND THE INQUIRY METHOD

A major instructional focus of teaching with primary sources throughout the modules is the emphasis on using inquiry learning to develop students' analytical thinking skills. As students interact with the photographs and other documents or artifacts, they relate the primary sources to their prior knowledge, to content they are currently studying, and to events happening around them. In the "Book Backdrops" unit, teachers begin with a work of literature and use resources from the Library of Congress to deepen students' understanding of the work and of the time when it was written. The example used is a children's book, *Mr. Lincoln's Whiskers*, written and illustrated by Karen B. Winnick (Boyds Mill Press, 1996). In the list of strategies at the end of the module, teachers will find not only suggestions for using Winnick's book, but how to create their own "Book Backdrop" from another work associated with their own curriculum.

*Mr. Lincon's Whiskers* is the true story of Grace Bedell, who wrote a letter to President Lincoln advising him to grow a beard after she had noticed how sad he looked in his 1860 campaign literature. Grace writes her letter to the president describing a shadow on the picture resembling a beard. She feels this "shadow beard" makes him look less sad, so she encourages him to grow a beard. President Lincoln actually answered her letter and visited her hometown—Springfield, Illinois—on a campaign stop. He requested her by name to come to the train and asked, "How do you like the improvement you advised me to make?"[2]

The original letters are in the Library of Congress collection and available as primary source documents for this lesson. The unit includes campaign literature, memorabilia, and photographs of Lincoln before and after growing the beard. With presidential campaign information widely available, comparing Lincoln's election campaign with recent presidential campaigns will bring the lesson right into the twenty-first century. Discussing the impact a young person's opinion might have on the look or style of the candidate could prove very interesting. There are no right or wrong answers. The objective is for students to make thoughtful, reflective connections between the past and present by formulating good questions and responding to them.

To extend the lesson and follow up on questions about Lincoln or his campaign, the exhibition website is still available (fig. 3.8). The "Book Backdrops" module provides a list of seventeen documents, photographs, and artifacts for students to study along with the reading of Winnick's book. The artifact shown on the web page is a campaign button showing Lincoln clean shaven (fig. 3.9). Perhaps Grace Bedell saw the same likeness before writing her letter.

FIGURE 3.9
*Abraham Lincoln–Hannibel Hamlin Campaign Button for 1860 presidential election.* Liljenquist Family Collection of Civil War Photographs, Library of Congress.

FIGURE 3.8
Screen capture of Library of Congress exhibit *With Malice Toward None*, created for the Abraham Lincoln Bicentennial Exhibition.

Students reading *Mr. Lincoln's Whiskers* are often fascinated that the president of the United States would take time to write to a little girl and that he may actually have grown a beard because she suggested it. The two students pictured below are reading Winnick's book and looking at pictures of Lincoln had no memory of him without a beard before reading this book (fig. 3.10). Even as high school students, they found the story engaging and wanted to learn more.

---

### CREATING A "BOOK BACKDROP" USING THE INQUIRY METHOD

To create a "Book Backdrop" for another literary work, the following suggestions are provided in the "Build and Deliver" module:

- **Content.** Select a topic(s) you will be studying in your classroom. Check your state and local school district standards and curriculum guides for content and skills suggestions.

- **Learning objective.** Determine what you want students to learn from working with the primary sources associated with the book you select. What is the enduring understanding?

- **Book selection.** Choose a book that aligns with your topic and is appropriate for your grade level. Consult online resources and booklists if necessary.

- **Pre-reading.** Before reading the book as a class, discuss its historical setting. Brainstorm words and events related to that time period.

- **Read.** As you (students) read the book, compile a list of dates, people, and events that might have primary source connections. (Teaching tip: use sticky notes while reading.) After reading, brainstorm again to extend vocabulary list.

- **Investigate.** Search the Library of Congress site for primary source items that connect with the selected book. Record findings (caption, collection, and permanent URL) on tracking sheet or another graphic organizer.

- **Share.** Share findings with class. Discuss how the primary sources that were found might increase student understanding of the book and its historical setting.

- **Question.** Discuss further learning possibilities. Discuss possible resources for more information Ask more questions. Look for more answers.[3]

Under "Teaching Strategies," thirteen creative lesson ideas are outlined to engage students in a deeper understanding of their book and the primary sources identified with the story. The strategies include having students use the facts and images they discover as a catalyst to write their own story or sequel to the story. Students might create their own "primary source" such as a "found poem" or letter. They could write a news article from the time period or add lyrics to a song. Photographs are tremendous story starters as students imagine what is happening in the picture and the story behind each person or object in the photograph or painting. Different artists often portray the same event from different perspectives. There are no right or wrong answers when analyzing primary sources. Making connections between books and primary sources give inquisitive minds opportunities to stretch in new and inventive directions bringing literature and history alive for young readers.

---

Source: Library of Congress, OC Educational Outreach Division, "Book Backdrops," *TPS Direct: Teaching with Primary Sources*, 19.

To help teachers create their own "Book Backdrops," a graphic organizer is provided to identify and sort a variety of primary sources that will relate to the keywords in the story or text (fig. 3.11).

After completing "Staff Development" modules from "Build and Deliver" and viewing the online training videos, you are ready to investigate other lesson and professional development opportunities available from the "Teachers" page. Check out the bottom of the "Professional Development" web page (fig. 3.12) for links to more training oppor-

FIGURE 3.10
Students read Karen Winnick's book *Mr. Lincoln's Whiskers*, and library books filling in background information on the period and providing photographs of Lincoln without a beard.
Photograph by Katharine Lehman.

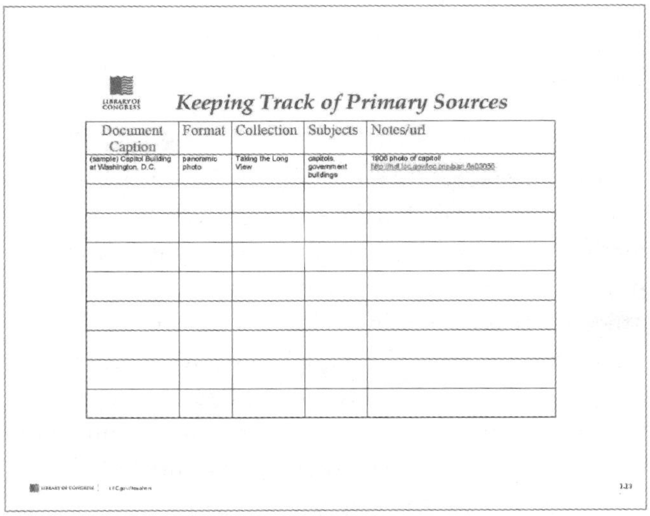

FIGURE 3.11
Screen capture of "Keeping Track of Primary Sources" from the TPS module "Book Backdrops."

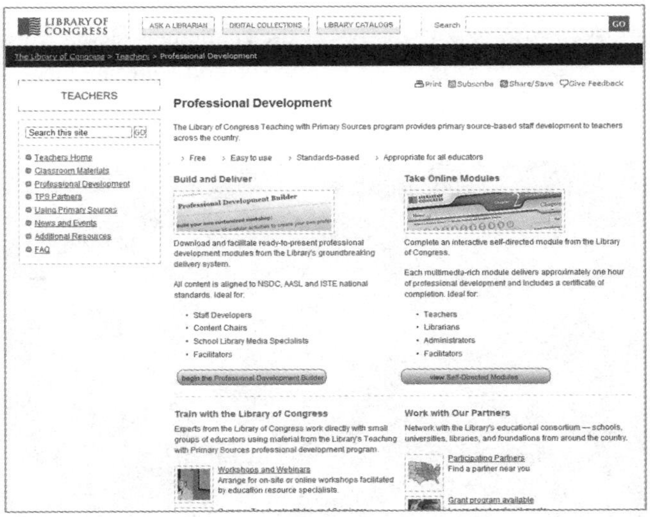

FIGURE 3.12
Screen capture of the lower section of the "Professional Development" page from the "Teachers" page of the Library of Congress website.

tunities. In-house training workshops at the library and videoconference opportunities with Library of Congress staff for live workshops in your home district are just two of the possibilities listed. All are free.

## TEACHING WITH PRIMARY SOURCE PARTNERS: FIND A PARTNER NEAR YOU

Throughout the United States, regional partners are developing programs to train and model the use of primary sources in the classroom. Grants are available to develop new programs for those interested in pursuing or improving partnerships in their geographic area. The Library of Congress website has a wealth of information on how to find out about partnerships in your area and how to apply for grants on the "Teachers" page (see the link "Grant program available" on fig. 3.12). To learn about specific success stories, check out the *Teaching with Primary Sources Journal*. To find a list of university programs affiliated with the Library of Congress teaching program, click on the consortium member list linked from the "Participating Partners" link (shown in fig. 3.12). Most have a "Consortium Member Showcase" link under their name.

   As an example of the timely subjects highlighted in the journal, formerly named the *Teaching with Primary Sources Quarterly*, look at the Spring 2010 issue in the archives focusing on project-based learning. Consortium members and TPS mentors have submitted articles on this theme showing how students can use primary sources to focus on real-world applications that are both authentic and relevant in today's classroom. The feature article by Kathleen Ferenz defines project-based learning and gives examples through case studies. In one study, students analyzing photographs of child labor gain knowledge of the historical context that gave rise to the challenges of American industrialization. Guided by the teacher's questions, students come to understand how citizens helped solve the challenges facing America at that time. Students apply this new knowledge to today's world and generate ideas of how citizens might apply similar strategies to meet challenges in our society.[3]

FIGURE 3.13
*Enlargement of Waynesburg, Greene County, PA, 1897.*
Library of Congress Geography and Map Division.

For elementary students, the project-based lesson is for grades 4–6. "Investigating the Building Blocks of Our Community's Past, Present and Future" was submitted by Andrea Buchanan, a participant in the TPS program at Waynesburg University in Pennsylvania. Students begin analyzing a historic map of their community found in the Library of Congress collections (fig. 3.13). Buchanan describes how "the class develops a plan for investigating how their local community's built environment reflects its past, present and future."[4]

   After studying the map and comparing their current knowledge of the town to the buildings in 1897, students come to a better understanding of changes in their community and predict how new changes will be made in the future. Extension activities include taking a historic walking tour of their community and hosting an event to share their new knowledge of the community.

The secondary lesson focuses on attitudes toward immigration and the role songs can play in voicing public opinion. In "Understanding Immigration through Popular Culture," students analyze several pieces of sheet music and listen to sound recordings to help them understand how new social patterns emerged at the turn of the twentieth century as a result of immigration. The song "Don't Bite the Hand That's Feeding You" by Jimmie Morgan, lyrics by Thomas Hoier (1916; figs. 3.14 and 3.15), provides insight into attitudes of that era, which in turn helps students better understand different views about immigration today. Meeting US history and music content standards, teachers guide students to recognize how "new social patterns, conflicts and ideas of national unity developed amid growing cultural diversity" and "the relationship between music, history and culture."[5]

The journal article is linked to a five-page PDF lesson plan filled with links to the sheet music, live recordings, images of immigrants, guides to analyzing manuscripts, and other primary sources. The accompanying primary source set, "Immigration Challenges for New Americans," is filled with background materials and tools to guide student analysis.

All the lessons provided through the *Teaching with Primary Sources Quarterly* and the new *TPS Journal* provide online links to additional resources and printable lesson plans in PDF format. These outstanding lessons cover all levels and content areas. They may be used as examples in staff development workshops and for teachers looking for specific lesson ideas to correlate with their state and national standards. Past themes include Critical

FIGURE 3.14 (Bottom left) Cover from "Don't Bite the Hand That's Feeding You/ Jimmie Morgan [notated Music]." Historic Sheet Music Collection, Library of Congress.

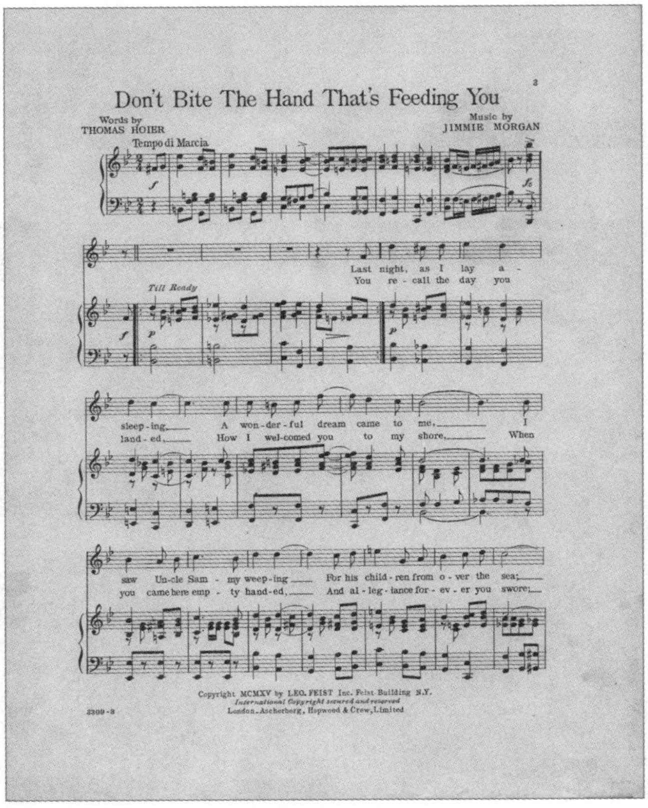

FIGURE 3.15 (Bottom right) First page of lyrics from "Don't Bite the Hand That's Feeding You/ Jimmie Morgan [notated Music]." Historic Sheet Music Collection, Library of Congress.

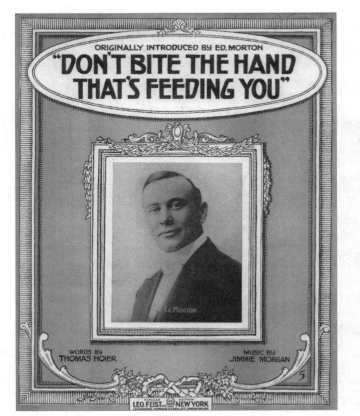

FIGURE 3.16
*[Addie Card,] Anemic Little Spinner in North Pownal Cotton Mill, Vermont, 1910.* Photograph by Lewis Wicks Hine. Library of Congress Prints and Photographs Division.

Thinking, Differentiated Instruction, English Language Learners, Historical Thinking, Inquiry Learning, Literacy Integration, Science, and Technology Integration.

## SUMMARY

As teachers begin using primary sources with students, the capacity of these sources to engage learners quickly becomes evident. The penetrating gazes of two children staring into the camera lens are stark examples of how primary sources become windows into the past (figs. 3.16 and 3.17). Analyzing these images, students literally see the challenges and infer the obstacles facing immigrant families and children in the push to build new lives and industrialize America at the turn of the twentieth century. Describing what they see, formulating questions about what they wonder, and researching answers to their questions, students gain greater understanding and knowledge of a bygone era that remains imprinted in their minds long after lecture notes have disappeared. Students apply the knowledge learned through these examples, and thus become more informed citizens with a deeper understanding of the challenges Americans face today and will face tomorrow.

FIGURE 3.17
*"Carrying-in" Boy in Alexandria Glass Factory, Alexandria, Va., 1911.* Photograph by Lewis Wicks Hine. Library of Congress Prints and Photographs Division.

## NOTES

1. Library of Congress, *TPS Direct: Teaching with Primary Sources*, PDF, December 9, 2010, iv.
2. Karen B. Winnick, *Mr. Lincoln's Whiskers* (Honesdale, PA: Boyds Mill Press, 1996), unp.
3. Kathleen Ferenz, "Project-Based Learning with Primary Sources," *Teaching with Primary Sources Quarterly* 3, no. 2 (Spring 2010), 2, www.loc.gov/teachers/tps/quarterly/project _learning/article.html.
4. Andrea Buchanan, "Investigating the Building Blocks of Our Community's Past, Present and Future," *Teaching with Primary Sources Quarterly* 3, no. 2 (Spring 2010), 6, www.loc.gov/teachers/tps/quarterly/project_learning/activity.html.
5. "Understanding Immigration through Popular Culture," *Teaching with Primary Sources Quarterly* 3, no. 2 (Spring 2010), 7, www.loc.gov/teachers/tps/quarterly/project_learning/pdf/ secondary_activity.pdf.

## BIBLIOGRAPHY

*[Abraham Lincoln-Hannibel Hamlin Campaign Button for 1860 Presidential Election].* Digital image. Liljenquist Family Collection of Civil War Photographs, Library of Congress Prints and Photographs Division. www.loc.gov/pictures/resource/ ppmsca.31540.

Buchanan, Andrea. "Investigating the Building Blocks of Our Community's Past, Present and Future." *Learning Activity, Elementary Level. Teaching with Primary Sources Quarterly* 3, no. 2. (Spring 2010): 6. www.loc.gov/teachers/tps/quarterly/project_learning/activity2.html.

"'Don't Bite the Hand That's Feeding You' / Jimmie Morgan [notated Music]: Sheet Music Brief Display: Performing Arts Encyclopedia, Library of Congress." Historic Sheet Music Collection—Library of Congress. http://lcweb2.10c.gov/diglib/ihas/loc.natlib. ihas.100007833.

Ferenz, Kathleen. "Project-Based Learning with Primary Sources." *Teaching with Primary Sources Quarterly* 3, no. 2 (Spring 2010): 2–4. www.loc.gov/teachers/tps/quarterly/project _learning.

Hine, Lewis Wicker. *Dotheboys Hall in Session. Location: Huntsville, Alabama.* 1913. Digital image. Library of Congress Prints and Photographs Division. www.loc.gov/ pictures/item/nc12004004068/PP.

Hine, Louis Wickes. *[Addie Card,] Anaemic Little Spinner in North Pownal Cotton Mill. See Photo No. 1056. Location: Vermont, 1910.* Digital image. Library of Congress Prints and Photographs Division. www.loc.gov/pictures/item/nc12004001719/PP.

Hine, Louis Wickes. *"Carrying-in" Boy in Alexandria Glass Factory, Alexandria, Va. 1911.* Digital image. Library of Congress Prints and Photographs Division. www.loc.gov/pictures/ item/nc12004002963/PP.

Library of Congress website. www.loc.gov/index.html.

*Lincoln Portrait, ca. 1858. From With Malice Toward None* exhibition. Library of Congress. Accessed July 18, 2013, http://myloc.gov/Exhibitions/lincoln/vignettes/CandidateLincoln/ ExhibitObjects/LincolnPortrait.aspx. or http://myloc.gov/Exhibitions/lincoln.

"[Map] Waynesburg, Greene County, Pennsylvania, 1897." Library of Congress Geography and Map Division Washington, DC. www.loc.gov/item/75696554.

"Professional Development—Overview." Library of Congress. www.loc.gov/teachers/professionaldevelopment.

"Professional Development Builder." Library of Congress. www.loc.gov/teachers/professionaldevelopment/tpsdirect/pdplanbuilder.

"Take Online Modules—Professional Development." Library of Congress. www.loc.gov/teachers/professionaldevelopment.

*Teaching with Primary Sources: Professional Development: Analyzing Photographs*. PDF. Washington, DC: Library of Congress Outreach Division, December 9, 2010.

*Teaching with Primary Sources: Professional Development: Book Backdrops*. PDF. Washington, DC: Library of Congress Educational Outreach Division, December 9, 2010.

*TPS Direct: Teaching With Primary Sources: Professional Development*. PDF. Washington, DC: Library of Congress Educational Outreach Division, December 9, 2010.

"Understanding Immigration through Popular Culture." *Teaching with Primary Sources Quarterly* 3, no. 2 (Spring 2010): 7. www.loc.gov/teachers/tps/quarterly/pdf/Spring2010SecondaryLevelLearningActivity.pdf.

"Using Primary Sources—Teachers." Library of Congress. www.loc.gov/teachers/usingprimarysources.

VanBrunt, Walter. "Don't Bite the Hand That's Feeding You." Recorded October 31, 1929. Jimmie Morgan. Library of Congress Motion Picture, Broadcasting and Recorded Sound Division. 1916. http://memory.loc.gov/mbrs/edrs/50357r.wav.

Winnick, Karen B. *Mr. Lincoln's Whiskers*. Honesdale, PA: Boyds Mill Press, 1996.

# Action Lessons:
# Interacting with History

COMPILED BY KATHARINE LEHMAN
FROM PARTICIPANTS OF THE 2011
LIBRARY OF CONGRESS SUMMER INSTITUTE

After being immersed in the Library of Congress web pages and inspired by the possibilities, you are invited in this chapter to move through a series of classroom activities showing students actively interacting with history through primary sources. The following lesson plans were created by participants of the Summer Institute and completed successfully in classrooms across the country. Some lessons were created at the Library of Congress as part of the weeklong program. Some were adapted from the institute plans, and others were created within the teacher's content area back in their home school. All exemplify best practices in the classroom and model strategies to energize classroom learning with remarkable resources available to educators through the Library of Congress.

Figure 4.1
Students analyze primary sources with a "historian in residence" in Teresa St. Angelo's kindergarten classroom. Photograph by Teresa St. Angelo.

## ELEMENTARY BEGINNINGS

## MONTHLY VISITS WITH A HISTORIAN

Kindergarten teacher Teresa St. Angelo from John I. Dawes —Early Learning Center in Manalapan-Englishtown, New Jersey, arranged monthly visits with a "historian in residence" (fig. 4.1). Her historian is actually a parent volunteer who guides small groups of students as they examine a photograph or print and answer questions St. Angelo compiles to help students connect primary sources with the content theme of the month. To introduce the yearlong concept of resident historian and primary sources,

September's study begins with the Library of Congress, the Reading Room, and the job of a historian. In October students compare a print of a Mayan shell used to call the community to gather for news with a megaphone and a Hawaiian shell. After the small-group activities, students share their initial discoveries with the whole class, then participate in a follow-up art or writing activity to assess what they learned and what they want to learn.

Other activities include comparing a First Thanksgiving painting and a photo of the 1942 Landis Farm Thanksgiving. In December students compare toy catalogs from 1887 and the present. While studying time in January, students analyze a photo of a clockmaker. After discovering what occupation the photo depicts, students write entries into a journal for a week as though they are a clockmaker. Coordinating with a local contest sponsored by a judge in February, students study photographs of the Supreme Court building and the Supreme Court justices. Students describe their concept of what justices do. In March, students study wind and weather. The historian brings a picture of Benjamin Franklin flying a kite (fig. 4.2).

Figure 4.2
*Franklin's Experiment with the Kite, 1911*. Photograph by Charles E Mills.
Library of Congress Prints and Photographs Division.

St. Angelo writes,

> They were amazed to realize Ben Franklin knew George Washington! It was hard to see what was at the end of the kite string without a magnifying glass but once they discovered the key in small group with their magnifying glasses, they were so excited!
>
> Creating each monthly lesson involved research on the Library of Congress website for material to match our unit of study. For example, in April, the theme was 'Wheels.' I sought primary sources by typing in *wheels*, then *bicycles*, and finally *tricycles* in the search bar. Finding the following primary source [fig. 4.3], I was confident the students would be interested and involved.
>
> I began to develop questions the students would consider through observation and reflection as outlined on the primary analysis tool. Describing how the students know the photo is from the past is an important part of every monthly lesson. The objective was for the students to realize the man was riding a tricycle and to explain why we need wheels.

> I made six copies of the photo. Each copy was attached to a clipboard. Magnifying glasses were placed on a table next to each clipboard. Students were called up to the table by a volunteer parent, and they were instructed to make their own observations and answer questions. Students worked in small groups of two or three.
>
> After students made their observations and reflections in a small group with the volunteer parent, we came together as a large group, sitting in a carpeted area. The photo was displayed on our smartboard. Each student had an opportunity to come to the smartboard to describe and circle what they noticed in the photo.[1]

To ensure parent involvement with each lesson, St. Angelo prepared a question sheet to be sent home (see "History in Our Class").

Figure 4.3
*Baum, Geo. L., Captain, Nov. 18, 1919.*
Library of Congress Prints and Photographs Division.

HISTORY IN OUR CLASS

(Where the past comes alive!)

**Dear Parents:**
**Your child analyzed the attached photograph of a tricycle!**

Following are the questions they had to think about and answer:

1. What do you see in the picture?
2. What else?
3. What is the man riding?
4. How many wheels do you see?
5. What do you think his job is?
6. Is this an old picture?
7. How do you know?
8. Do you see any cars?
9. Describe what they look like.
10. How are they different than your family car?
11. Do you think this man ever drove a car?

I have included some information about the bicycles! Hope you enjoy!
And . . . have fun asking your child what he/she learned today![2]

Source: Teresa St. Angelo, "Using Primary Sources in Kindergarten," e-mail message to author, April 9, 2012.

Teresa St. Angelo's kindergarten students completed an entire year interacting with primary sources through their interaction with the "resident historian" and analysis of a variety of photographs, prints, and artifacts. Most important, St. Angelo writes, "questioning and thinking skills grew with each month. Students began to carry over their questioning and inquiry skills into their science and literacy work. Their sense of history, purpose, and curiosity grew along with their vocabulary and analyzing skills."[3] In each lesson, students connected the resources with similar objects, holidays, concepts, and events in their present lives.

PRIMARY SOURCES USED WITH A HISTORIAN
THROUGHOUT THE SCHOOL YEAR

September | The Library of Congress and the Reading Room
www.loc.gov/pictures/item/2011632501
www.loc.gov/pictures/item/2011646837

October | "Calling People to Gather"
• Mayan shell from the Exploring the Early Americas exhibition, "Ritual, Ceremonies and Celebrations."
  www.loc.gov/exhibits/exploring-the-early-americas/virtual-ceremonies-and
  -celebrations.html

## PRIMARY SOURCES USED WITH A HISTORIAN THROUGHOUT THE SCHOOL YEAR
### (Continued)

### November | Thanksgiving
- Print of "The First Thanksgiving 1621" by Jean Leon Gerome Ferris. www.loc.gov/pictures/item/2001699850

- Photograph of "Neffsville, Pennsylvania. Thanksgiving Dinner at the House of Earle Landis, 1942," by Marjory Collins. www.loc.gov/pictures/item/owi2001014451/PP

### December
- Toy catalog page, "Advertisement for Pictorial Toy Catalogue No. 2 [showing composite of many toys on shelves], Jan 1887" Library of Congress Prints and Photographs Division www.loc.gov/pictures/item/2004672357

*From the Library of Congress home page, users can quickly narrow their search. In the right search box, enter the keywords in the title of a print, object, or photograph. Match keywords with the format in the left drop menu. If you are unsure of the format, leave the default "all formats" (fig. 4.4).*

Figure 4.4
Screen capture of the Library of Congress home page showing a sample search with keywords "Der Uhrmacher" combined with the format "Photo, Print, Drawing."

### January
- The clockmaker, "Der Uhrmacher," a print that shows a man making a small clock in a clock-making shop between 1840 and 1890. Library of Congress Prints and Photographs Division www.loc.gov/pictures/item/2009631807/resource

### February
- U.S. Supreme Court Building, U.S. Supreme Court Justices. Library of Congress Prints and Photographs Division www.loc.gov/pictures/resource/highsm.17863 www.loc.gov/pictures/item/2003668576

### March | Benjamin Franklin
- Mills, Charles E. *Franklin's Experiment with the Kite, 1911*. Library of Congress Prints and Photographs Division www.loc.gov/pictures/resource/cph.3b42841

### April
- Mailman on wheels, Captain George Baum, Library of Congress Prints and Photographs Division www.loc.gov/pictures/item/npc2007000768

## THINK, PUZZLE, AND EXPLORE WITH MAPS

Figure 4.5
Third-grade students study a
section of Martin Waldseemüller's
1507 world map projected from
the Library of Congress website.
Photograph by Jennifer Burgin.

Third-grade teacher Jennifer Burgin returned from the Summer Institute inspired to introduce her Arlington, Virginia, students to historic maps from the 1500s and 1600s (fig. 4.5). These maps are a natural fit into the Virginia social studies curriculum which requires teachers to use primary sources. As well as looking closely at details and analyzing what they see, students in this unit are encouraged to reflect about the mind sets and perspectives of famous early explorers from Europe to the Americas. Particularly helpful was the interactive site referenced in chapter 1, the 1507 Waldseemüller map (see fig. 1.17). Using the Library of Congress Digital World Library site to zoom in on sections of the map, students compare the original drawing with what they know of the world today.

Using the "think, puzzle, explore" strategy, students begin their study with a pre-quiz to establish their level of understanding. Individually they reply to the question "What do you think explorers knew about America in the 1400s?" with the statement, "I think . . . because . . ." Burgin divides the class into six groups and gives each group a section of the map showing what was known of North America. Students use their eyes to silently explore their piece of the map and share within their group what they notice. Using the Primary Source Analysis Tool (fig. 2.17), the group records their ideas and wonders or "puzzles" about their section of the map. If a group needs prompting Burgin will walk around and offer these questions:

1. What do you see?
2. What on this map looks strange and unfamiliar?
3. What on this map do you recognize?
4. What, if any, words do you see?

Burgin continues by stating aloud, "As a group decide what you think this is a map of. If you cannot decide upon one idea, share the ideas that you collectively come up with."[4]

Together the class will make comparisons between what they discovered in their groups and maps of the world today. Questions include:

1. What is the same?
2. What is different?
3. What does the map reveal about the people who used this map?
4. What does this map make us wonder?

The second map analyzed by students to compare with the 1507 Waldseemüller map was printed about a hundred years later, in 1606, by Willem Janszoon Blaeu in Amsterdam. Much more had been discovered about the New World in the intervening years. Students can pick out many familiar place names from the Latin such as Virginia, Florida, California, and Sinus Mexicanus. The skill of early cartographers to draw the world as accurately as they did is truly amazing; students become immersed in discovering similarities and differences between historic and modern maps of the Americas. Reflecting on what they observe and recognizing the similarities and differences in the maps, students are stimulated to learn and understand more about geography and how our knowledge of the world has evolved.

---

**PART 2 FROM JENNIFER BURGIN'S ANALYZING MAPS LESSON PLAN: INTRODUCING THE BLAEU MAP**

I. **Review of the Waldseemüller map (1507)**
   - Call students to the Smartboard area and review what we did yesterday.
   - Ask the students what people thought of the world in the 1400s and what they think of the world today.
   - If the class was unable to look at the updated Waldseemüller map (1516), then take a brief look at that; explain how some people thought that others were not ready to accept another continent.
   - Look at the 1507 Waldseemüller map and "take" a mental snap shot of it, especially focusing on what was "North America."

II. **Introduction to the Blaeu map (1606) [fig. 4.6]**
   - Show the Blaeu map. Give a brief introduction to the time frame (the 1600s) of the map and figure out as a class how much time has passed from the Waldseemüller map to the Blaeu map. Explain that by the 1600s there had been more voyages to the "New World," and more information had been gathered about what we now call North America.
   - Ask the students to describe only what they see.
   - Ask the students to ask questions about the Blaeu map.
   - Ask students to reflect upon the Blaeu map and make decisions about it ("I think . . . because . . .")

III. **Compare-and-Contrast Activity**
   - Lay out a paper copy of the Waldseemüller map from the day before and leave the Blaeu map on the Smartboard.
   - Guide the students to answer at least one point for each of the three parts of the Venn diagram. (Draw a classic Venn diagram of two overlapping circles creating three sections with the center overlapping section used to list the common features of both maps.)
   - Have the students fill out Venn diagrams on their own or in clusters.
   - Have the students share their Venn diagram reflections with the class.
   - The teacher takes notes on the reflections on his or her own Venn diagram so that the students may collect these notes.

IV. **Time for Puzzling**
   - Ask the students what they wonder from seeing these two maps.
   - Ask the students what they think would happen if they showed today's maps to the people of the 1500s and the 1600s.
   - Ask the students how they think maps have changed and why they have changed.

V. **Activity Assessment—how will you measure student mastery of the learning objectives?**
   - Does the student participate and engage in asking questions and observing?
   - Does the student note the differences in maps and human knowledge as time moves on?
   - Can the student express why maps change over time?

---

Source: Jennifer Burgin, "Primary Sources Project Plan Outline: Teaching with Primary Sources," Library of Congress Summer Institute, Summer 2011, 4–5.

Jennifer Burgin wrote:

> When I taught the geography and famous explorers unit to my students, I utilized the in-depth lesson plans I created; I also invited one of my institute teachers and her colleague to come view and interact with the students and myself while teaching the lesson and received feedback from them on the practices and instruction I demonstrated.
>
> The students' responses to my questions and energetic comments lead me to believe that this lesson was inspiring and engaging; days later the children were still asking questions such as "Was that map used by the Ancient Chinese?" and "Why did the map look like it was shaped like a jellybean?" All of my students participated in the activity through offering comments, writing down notes on an analysis sheet, and critically observing the map.[5]

The impact of using primary sources with her students has had a profound impact on Burgin's teaching style. She writes,

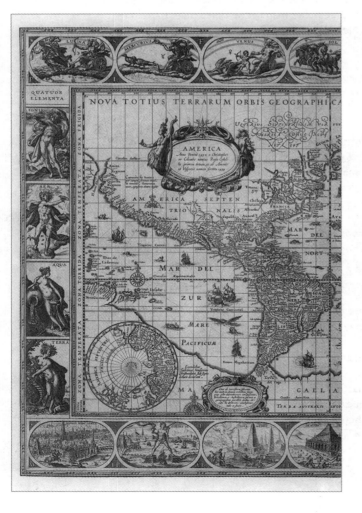

FIGURE 4.6
Detail from Willem Janszoon Blaeu's *Nova Totius Terrarum Orbis Geographica Ac Hydrographica Tabula [1606]*. Library of Congress American Memory Map Collection.

> Before, I might occasionally use a photograph from the LOC's database or another accredited source; now, however, I've been taught how to search for primary sources, how to determine the effectiveness of a source, and how to implement the sources in my classroom not only for supporting a lesson but also for digging deeply into the curriculum. I am using primary sources (photographs, video and sound recordings, digital copies of manuscripts, etc.) in innovative ways such as supporting language arts read aloud books and introducing robust vocabulary words. For example, a few months ago I read a story to the children from our curriculum about how televisions became popular over many decades. To show how the world received media before television, I found two primary sources from the LOC's website. One was a sound clip of a radio recording of an actress reading aloud the story of "Goldilocks and the Three Bears"; the other was a silent filming of Annie Oakley performing her famous sharp shooting for an audience.
>
> The institute taught me how to truly use the "observe and reflect" method with my class, but it also integrated a third part of asking why when finishing a reflection. I ask students now during my lessons to share what they see without assumptions; afterward we begin to reflect upon what we saw and then draw conclusions.[6]

MATERIALS FOR THE "HISTORIC MAP" LESSON

- 1 copy (cut into 12 pieces) of the Waldseemüller map (circa 1507) http://hdl.loc.gov/loc.gmd/g3200.ct000725

- 1 copy (cut into 4 pieces) of the Blaeu map (circa 1606) http://hdl.loc.gov/loc.gmd/g3200.ct001217v

- Primary Source Analysis Tool (1 per student, double-sided copy; one side is for each map)

- 1 enlarged copy (printed or handmade) of the Primary Source Analysis Tool (for teacher use)

- writing tools (colorful markers preferred) for writing on the larger copy of the Primary Source Analysis Tool

- copies of blank Venn diagrams (one per student or cluster, plus one for the teacher to record class reflections)

**What do you think explorers knew about America in the 1400s?**

I think

_____

_____

because

_____

_____

FIGURE 4.7
*1753—Washington Crossing the Allegheny.*
Painting by Carl Rakeman.
Federal Highway Administration, US Department of Transportation.

# ORQ CHARTS— OBSERVE, REFLECT, QUESTION

As a traveling resource teacher in Garrett County Public School, Oakland, Maryland, Sandy Rodeheaver uses primary sources from the Library of Congress as "hooks" for students to build base knowledge in the classroom. She guides students to analyze the resources with ORQ charts provided on the teacher pages of the Library of Congress website (see figs. 2.17 and 2.18). Her students "observe what they see, make connections to themselves through reflection and construct questions to explore."[7] Looking at three renditions depicting a young George Washington crossing the Allegheny River, students observe that there is another young man in the pictures (fig. 4.7). Once the other gentleman is identified, the essential questions to pursue become, "Who was Christopher Gist, and what was his relationship with George Washington?" In small groups armed with magnifying glasses, students move through a three-part process to observe, wonder, and reflect about what they see.

**GRADE LEVEL**
*Fourth*

**SUBJECT AREA**
*Maryland history,*
*Pre–French and*
*Indian War, historical*
*characters present*
*in local area*

**TOPIC**
*The relationship*
*of a young*
*George Washington*
*and Christopher Gist*

# PRIMARY SOURCE PROJECT OUTLINE PLAN— GEORGE WASHINGTON CROSSING THE ALLEGHENY RIVER

## Defining and Measuring Activity and Goals

**Essential Question:**
What big ideas do you want students to explore through this activity?

- Who was Christopher Gist, and what was his relationship with George Washington?

### Learning Objectives

What content and critical thinking skills do you want students to acquire and be able to perform as a result of this activity?

Students will be able to:

- Analyze pictures/portraits of Christopher Gist with George Washington
- Express ideas and questions about the images
- Create questions to investigate
- Compare pictures/portraits
- Write a headline of the event depicted

### Activity Assessment

How will you measure student mastery of the learning objectives?

- Using the photograph, observing, and using their prior knowledge, students will complete the "Analyzing Primary Sources" worksheet in small groups. On their exit card, they will then create a "headline" for their primary document.
- Students will compare their questions about these two men to questions generated in the other groups.

## Activity Plan

**Materials:**
What materials will you need to implement this activity?

- 3 prints of George Washington and Christopher Gist on the raft on the Alleghany River in December of 1753.
    - http://hdl.loc.gov/loc.pnp/cph.3a43166
    - www.fhwa.dot.gov/rakeman/1753.htm
    - www.picturehistory.com/product/id/137
    - http://oldstonehousepa.org/2009/09/29/now-available-the-journals-of-george-washington-christopher-gist-mission-to-fort-le-boeuf

(The last two are the same photo, but the first has the information, and the next is a better copy of the image.)

- "Analyzing Primary Sources" worksheet
- pencils
- magnifying glass
- chart paper
- markers
- interactive whiteboard

## Engage
### Background Knowledge
What do students need to know in order to successfully participate in this activity?
- Students will need to be familiar with the observe/reflect/question procedure.
- Students will be able to use a magnifying glass.

### Activating Background Knowledge
How will you activate students' background knowledge?

Part I: "Observe, Reflect, Question" (15 minutes)
1. Hand each student group one of the three prints.
2. Allow one minute to quietly observe image (fourteen minutes for this next section below).
3. Ask the students to write their observations to the question "What do you see in the image?"
4. Ask the students to reflect and write their thoughts about what they see.
5. Ask the students to write any questions they may have about who the men are and what they are doing.

Part II: "Observe, Reflect, Question" (15 minutes)
1. As a group put pictures up on the whiteboard for the whole class to see.
2. Have each group point out what they "observed, reflected, and questioned" about their picture.
3. Ask the students if they have more observations, reflections, and questions to write down.
4. Ask the students to return to their image and create a "headline" for the picture.

### The "Hook":
How will you introduce the activity and "hook" students' interest?
- Explain that during the trimester, the class will become historians. Their job is to use primary sources (e.g., prints, diaries) to explore how Garrett County's history played a part in building US history.

## Develop Critical Thinking Skills
### Activity Procedure:
Will you adapt an analysis activity you've experienced during the institute (e.g., photograph analysis)?
- Review with students the "right" and "wrong" way to use a magnifying glass.
- Explain that the class will be using magnifying glasses to perform an "observe, reflect, question" activity.
- Also explain that they will need to use both their prior knowledge and experience to fill in the worksheet with their group.
- Pass out the images to the groups and explain that they have one minute to look at the photo before they start to fill in the worksheet.
- Have students fill in the sheet together and actively share within their group.
- Ask the students to share what they have observed, reflected, and questioned with the whole class.
- Complete an "observe, reflect, question" sheet together as a class.
- Give time for students to add to their group sheets based on fellow students' information.

### Instructional Strategies

What instructional strategies will you use to help students build critical thinking skills (e.g., visible thinking, think-pair-share)?

- guided practice (will occur in previous lessons and reviewed with the group activity)
- visible thinking
- inquiry

### Questioning

What questions will you ask students to encourage deeper thinking (e.g., "What makes you say that?") When students share their observations, the teacher will:

- Frame students' observations by asking for certain things they noticed (e.g., details about the environment, clothing, and expressions of the two men).
- Ask students to point to their observations in the photograph or ask them to explain their thinking. This will help students begin to distinguish between observations and reflections.

### Construct Knowledge

After the activity of shared observations, the teacher will ask:

- Why do you think there were three different pictures of this event?
- Does it make you wonder who these men are?
- Where would we go to find the information you seek?

### Integrating Content

How will students move beyond their analysis in order to investigate their questions and construct new knowledge?

- Students will have access to other resources from this time period (e.g., diaries, artifacts, historical interpreters).
- At this time this is an open-ended activity. I am hoping that this lesson is an introduction to pique more curiosity about this era. I think it would be great for the students to create a final project to reflect their knowledge.

Source: Sandy Rodeheaver, "Primary Source Project Plan: Outline. Teaching with Primary Sources," Library of Congress. May 26, 2011:1–4.

Rodeheaver continues in her description prepared at the Summer Institute, "This lesson will follow several activities that involve using the "Observe, Reflect, Question" worksheet. This current activity will bring up many questions from students about the remaining person in the Gist images. I hope to introduce diary entries from George Washington as to who "Gist" is and how he relates to Garrett County and the US. This will be part of a whole unit on the period right before the French and Indian War."[8]

In her follow-up e-mail after teaching the unit, Rodeheaver remarks, "We did end up as a class reading the journals of Washington telling of the event. It was an event that cemented their friendship and was a precursor of how the two would work together during the French and Indian War."[9]

## MIDDLE SCHOOL BOOK CONNECTIONS

At Swan Meadow School, Rodeheaver has created a website for students in grades 6, 7, and 8 to connect books on the summer reading list with primary source prints and photographs in the Library of Congress collections. The titles highlighted in one Garrett County Summer Reading Program include *The War Horse* by Michael Morpurgo, *Children of the Lamp* by P. B. Kerr, *The Mostly True Adventures of Homer Figg Pig* by Rodman Philbrick, *The Hunger Games* by Suzanne Collins, *Blood on the River* by Eliza Carbone, and *The Picture of Hollis Woods* by Patricia Rilly Giff.[10] Each web page includes historic

FIGURE 4.8
*French Officers Watering Horses* [between ca. 1914 and ca. 1915]. Bain News Service. Library of Congress Prints and Photographs Division.

photographs, web links on the author, book reviews, and a brief summary of the book. A list of "read-alikes" on similar themes is also included. Extending the meaning of the books with primary sources adds another dimension to the study of these novels. When one class studied *The War Horse*, Rodeheaver directed a lesson having students use the OQR charts to analyze five photographs that illustrate use and care of horses in the war effort (fig. 4.8). Rodeheaver writes, "Students observe what they see, make connections to themselves through reflection and construct questions to explore. I can't ever say enough about the primary sources that are available from the Library of Congress and how easy I have found to slip them into a lesson on about anything."[11]

## SUGGESTED PHOTOGRAPHS OF WORLD WAR I FOR STUDENT ANALYSIS WHILE STUDYING THE WAR HORSES

Bain News Service. *French Officers Watering Horses*. Digital image. Library of Congress Prints and Photographs Division. Accessed May 24, 2012. www.loc.gov/pictures/item/ggb2005017385.

Bain News Service. *Paris—Horses Taken for War*. Digital image. Library of Congress Prints and Photographs Division. Accessed May 24, 2012. www.loc.gov/pictures/item/ggb2005017137.

Beam, George L. *Fort Logan World War I, 1917 or 1918*. Digital image [horse and rider]. Denver Public Library Digital Collections. Accessed May 24, 2012. http://cdm15330.contentdm.oclc.org/cdm/ref/collection/p15330c01122/id/32218.

Beam, George L. *Fort Logan World War I, 1917 or 1918*. Digital image [wagon]. Denver Public Library Digital Collections. Accessed May 24, 2012. http://cdm15330.contentdm.oclc.org/cdm/ref/collection/p15330c01122/id/32227.

Blue Cross Fund, London. *"Do Something" for the Horses—Help the Blue Cross Fund*. Digital image. Library of Congress Prints and Photographs Division. Accessed May 24, 2012. www.loc.gov/pictures/item/2003675258.

## VISUAL THINKING

*What is going on in this picture?*
*What makes you say that?*
*What more do you see?*[12]

In Montgomery County, Maryland, Krista McKim models the strategy of visual thinking in her eight-grade English class as students explore connections between primary sources and Conrad Richter's book *The Light in the Forest* (fig. 4.9). Analyzing photographs; etchings; paintings; and firsthand accounts of Native Americans, white captives, and early pioneers, students make observations to help them visualize the era and events in history that are contemporary with the setting of the novel.

In a journal article shared at the Summer Institute, "Making Thinking Visible," Ritchhart and Perkins explain the concepts of visible thinking that McKim models with her students. When students are encouraged to think through what they see, Ritchhart and Perkins find, they exhibit greater understanding of content and higher retention of that content. Guided by their teacher to question and think, students become more curious and open minded. Sharing ideas in social settings fosters opportunities for practicing reasoning skills and relating prior knowledge to the discussion. Students learn by "investigating rather than stockpiling facts."[13]

McKim believes the best part of using visual primary sources is that students can generate their own ideas of events about which they have no previous knowledge, making the process and the source more meaningful and engaging. For example, *The Light in the Forest* centers on the return of white captives that was part of a treaty negotiation in the 1700s between the Native Americans and Colonel Henry Bouquet. See figure 4.9 for a photo of students looking at a painting (fig. 4.10) of that event.

FIGURE 4.9
Ashley shares her perspective of a painting with her group members. Photograph by Krista McKim.

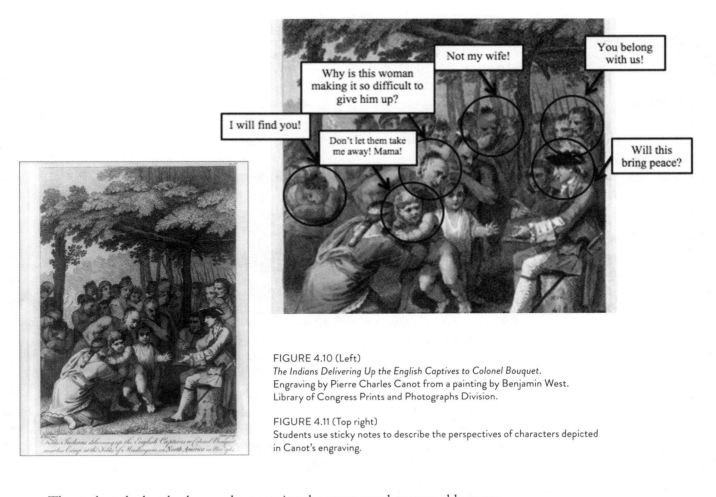

FIGURE 4.10 (Left)
*The Indians Delivering Up the English Captives to Colonel Bouquet.*
Engraving by Pierre Charles Canot from a painting by Benjamin West.
Library of Congress Prints and Photographs Division.

FIGURE 4.11 (Top right)
Students use sticky notes to describe the perspectives of characters depicted
in Canot's engraving.

The students had no background concerning the event, yet they were able to use visual thinking to uncover some of the essential facts regarding this event. Here is a sampling of the conversations:

**Student 1:** "The Indians are giving their children to the Americans."
**Student 2:** "Why would they give their kids to the Americans? I would never give up my kid."
**Student 3:** "Are they their children? The kids look white."
**Student 1:** "That's what I thought. Maybe they're giving the kids back."
**Student 2:** "Why do they have them in the first place?"[14]

Even though there are some factual misconceptions—the Native Americans were giving the white captives to the French, not the Americans—it didn't matter. The students had looked at the painting and become curious about the event. This made them more motivated to read *The Light in the Forest* and the primary source diaries of white captives. They generated their own questions, which they were to eventually answer using the book and diaries.

The students also worked in groups to look at different perspectives of the people in the painting. Below you will see a typed version of the assignment a group turned in (fig. 4.11). Please note that the original assignment used written sticky notes, but to make it easier to read here, the notes have been printed.

## PRIMARY SOURCE PROJECT PLAN OUTLINE: NATIVE AMERICANS

**GRADE LEVEL**
*Eighth*

**SUBJECT AREA**
*English*

**TOPIC**
*Native Americans*

### Essential questions

What is the truth of a situation?

How do different perspectives affect the definition of truth?

### Learning Objectives

Students will be able to:

- Generate questions related to white captives
- Analyze primary sources
- Compare primary source to a fictional account
- Analyze how perspective changes the concept of truth

### Final Activity Assessment

Students will work in groups to craft a PowerPoint comparing the primary sources to the text of *The Light in the Forest*.

### Materials

Promethean board or Smartboard to project *Indians Delivering Up Captives 1700s and Indians Walking in File 1833*

sticky notes

white captives etchings (six sets of the five paintings):

> *The Captivity of Mrs. Rowlandson 1857*
> www.loc.gov/pictures/item/95504883
> *The Captive White Boy 1886*
> www.loc.gov/pictures/item/2006682475
> *Indians Delivering Up Captives 1700s*
> www.loc.gov./pictures/item/2012647230
> *Indians Walking in File 1833*
> www.loc.gov/pictures/item/2001696054
> *A Scene on the Third Night of my Captivity 1871*
> www.loc.gov/pictures/item/2003663677

firsthand accounts of captives (selections)

> *Life of Mary Jemison, The White Woman of the Genesee 1860*
> Simple and direct text; only certain sections of the book were used.
> http://lccn.loc.gov/sd19000088
> *The American Pioneer 1844*
> On-level text; pages 42–56 of the magazine.
> http://lccn.loc.gov/04033614
> *Narrative of the Captivity and Restoration of Mrs. Mary Rowlandson 1794*
> Complex text, but the most humorous.
> http://lccn.loc.gov/20011344

## Day One

Students work in groups of five to six looking a set of the five images.

Analyze:

Each group has two to three minutes with each image discussing what is going on in the picture and what makes them say that. The questions they ask one another should be visual thinking/strategy based:

- What is going on in this picture?
- What makes you say that?
- What more do you see?

Analyze:

After looking at the five paintings, the students return to their seats and look at the following as a class:
- *Indians Delivering Up Captives 1700s*
- *Indians Walking in File 1833*

As a class they will share what they think is going on in these two pictures. These two pictures are of specific events that are referenced in *The Light in the Forest*.

Wonder:

On the board, we generate a list of questions we have regarding all the pictures. These questions are written on a class question wall, to be revisited while reading *The Light in the Forest*.

Synthesis:

Students pick one image to take the point of view of one of the characters in the photo or painting. What is that person thinking at that moment?

## Day Two

This is to be done after reading *The Light in the Forest*. Please note that we will be answering the questions on the class question wall as we read the book.

Analyze:

As a class, we begin by looking at the answers to the questions on the wall and discussing whether we can use *The Light in the Forest* as a source to answer these questions.

Analyze:

Students gather in groups of three. They are given a list of the questions they generated on day one and copies of selections from the three primary sources. Each student reads one of the three selections. They answer the questions based on the viewpoint of their captive narrative.

Share:

The students share their narrative with the other two students in their group.

Analyze:

On a sticky note, the students write, "I believe that (this narrative/text) is the best source of information because . . ."

## Day Three

Discuss:

As a class, students share their thoughts of the narratives, focusing on which one they feel is true. They discuss bias and background and how these elements influence the interpretations that the authors of the primary sources make.

Compare:

Using a T chart, the students compare the text and the narratives.

## Days Four and Five

Synthesis:

The students work together to create a PowerPoint grading Conrad Richter's historical accuracy in the book *The Light in the Forest*. They need to use evidence and to cite quotes correctly from the book and the narratives. If the students are unable to finish in class, they can finish the PowerPoint for homework.

Note: This lesson plan can also be used while reading *I Am Regina* by Sally M. Keehn.
Source: Krista McKim, "Primary Source Project Plan: Outline. Native Americans. Teaching with Primary Sources," Library of Congress, 2011.

When duplicating the lessons as designed in this chapter, readers will discover that some recommended prints are available only in full size at the Library of Congress. Participants at the Institute have full access for enlarging and printing that online access denies. In such cases, using the library as an indexing resource enables teachers to locate the needed image from other online or print sources.

*The Captive White Boy 1886* (fig. 4.12) is available from the Library of Congress in color or black-and-white and may be enlarged or printed for students to view on a screen or on paper. *Indians Walking in a File* is available only as a thumbnail online at the Library of Congress, which is too small for close scrutiny. (If you search *"Indians Walking in a File"* and *"digital print"* in any online search engine, such as Google, you will find online sources with a copy of the same print in full screen for real-time classroom viewing.)

The Library of Congress's online index and thumbnail previews provide a tremendous resource for educators to identify titles and source information for lessons, even though the user may need to locate copies of some images elsewhere for large-screen viewing with students. Through the variety of images identified for this lesson, students see artist renditions and photographers' prints of many children living with Native Americans. Using visual thinking, students determine the truths depicted in each situation. In their study of *The Light in the Forest*, they will be viewing images and situations through the lens of Conrad Richter's protagonist, who adopted the world view of the Native Americans who raised him. Students may raise more questions than answers as they ad-

FIGURE 4.12
*[The Captive White Boy, Santiago McKinn in Geronimo's Camp, with Group of Indians, Mostly Children, in Front of Partially Constructed Tent, before Geronimo's Surrender to Gen. Crook, March 27, 1886].* Photograph by C. S. Fly. Library of Congress Prints and Photographs Division.

dress their essential questions, "What is the truth of a situation?" and "How do different perspectives affect the definition of truth?"

## HIGH SCHOOL HISTORY CONNECTIONS

### THINKING LIKE A HISTORIAN

In his *Primary Sources Quarterly* article "Thinking Like a Historian," Sam Wineburg describes history class for many high school students as an exercise in memorizing facts and repeating them back on the test. By contrast, to historians, "history is an argument about what facts should or shouldn't mean. Even when historians are able to piece together the basic story of what happened, they rarely agree about what an event means or what caused it. Historians argue about the past's meaning and what it has to tell us in the present."[15] Teachers can use primary sources to bring a story to life—to shift students into seeing history not as a set of finite facts but as a narrative (or narratives) with multiple variables and missing pieces that influence the conclusions. Students become detectives piecing together the facts and wondering about the implications and possibilities for actual and alternative outcomes.

### RECONSTRUCTING THE PANAMA CANAL DECISION

Christine Rick's US history class at Thomas Dale High School in Chester, Virginia, analyzed a series of pictures, telegrams, letters, and original writings copied from the Library of Congress website and the Manuscript and Archives Division to piece together the events behind the June 1902 Congressional vote for the United States to build a canal in

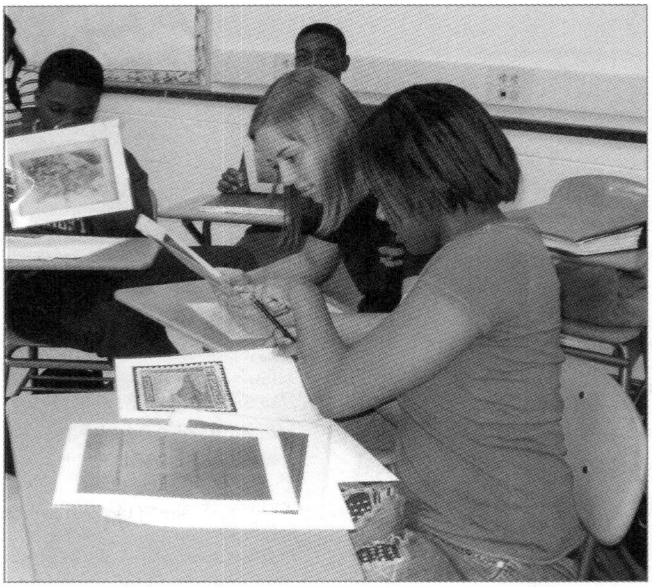

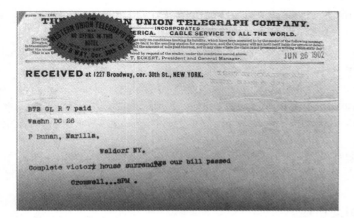

FIGURE 4.13
Students at Thomas Dale High School study primary sources related to the Panama Canal vote.
Photograph by Katharine Lehman.

THE ... N UNION TELEGRAPH COMPANY.
INCORPORATED
... ERICA. CABLE SERVICE TO ALL THE WORLD.

WESTERN UNION TELEGRAPH CO.
NO OFFICE IN THIS HOTEL
1227 B'WAY, Cor. 30th ST.

JUN 26 1902

R. C. CLOWRY, President and General Manager.

RECEIVED at 1227 Broadway, cor. 30th St., NEW YORK.

B78 GL R 7 paid
Washn DC 26
P Bunan, Warilla,
Waldorf NY.
Complete victory house surrenders our bill passed
Cromwell...SPM .

FIGURE 4.14
*Telegram from Philippe Bunau-Varilla Papers, 1877–1955.*
Cromwell to P. Bunau-Varilla. June 26, 1902.
Library of Congress Manuscripts Division.
Photographed by Katharine Lehman.

Panama instead of Nicaragua. As the collaborative lesson with school librarian Katharine Lehman began in February 2012, students were studying a unit on Teddy Roosevelt's administration and learning about the president's "big stick" foreign policies and imperialistic aspirations, which brought the Philippines, Hawaii, and Guam under US control. Was Panama to be next? Students would discover many facts leading up to the decision in the following exercise (fig. 4.13).

The behind-the-scenes political maneuverings by the French lobbyist Philippe Bunau-Varilla and his paid New York lobbyist, William Nelson Cromwell, were revealed in a series of letters, newspaper articles, brochures, telegrams, and pictures that were distributed in class. In small groups, students analyzed their individual pieces of the puzzle using the ORQ Primary Source Analysis Tool (fig. 2.17). A slideshow of the artifacts was projected in chronological order. Students explained their artifact as it was presented. Class discussion was opened up for students to decide each artifact's importance to the whole story. Did students discover everything that was happening that month in Congress? No. But the paper trail the Panama lobbyists left—along with newspaper stories and prior knowledge students had of President Roosevelt's personality and political policies—helped students understand what happens in Washington, how lobbyists work, and how tension mounts for a vote. There were no surprises when the final Panama telegram declares, "Complete Victory, house surrenders. Our bill passed." (See fig. 4.14.)

Was this the end of the story? Thinking like a historian, students have more parts of the puzzle to piece together. Was Columbia eager to let the United States finish the canal that France started? Who was behind the revolution in Panama to end Columbian dominance? What was Bunau-Varilla's role in the creation of the new government in Panama, the writing of their constitution, and the treaty that gave the US permission to build the canal? As students put the whole picture together, a pattern of intrigue and international political maneuvering emerges. Had Bunau-Varilla never mounted his lobbying effort, would there be a Panama Canal today?

The manuscript documents photocopied by Lehman at the Library of Congress during the Summer Institute substantiate Bunau-Varilla's involvement in the lobbying

FIGURE 4.15
*Roosevelt's Rough Diggers.*
Cartoon in *Puck*, November 14, 1906.
Library of Congress.

effort for the canal decision. Why did he do it? He never publically confesses. Celebrated historians such as David McCullough, who has written extensively on the subject, note that Bunau-Varilla—a failed French engineer on the original project—became a very wealthy man in his retirement years. When the United States bought out the French interests in the Canal, many French and foreign investors recouped their lost investments. Bunau-Varilla never admitted he worked for those who lost their money. He saw himself in the role of a "knight errant" doing his duty for his country.[16] Readers, it is your turn to "think like a historian" and put the missing pieces together and form your opinion in this matter. Was Bunau-Varilla's primary motivation to serve France? An important fact to remember when studying primary documents is that the answers are not always cut-and-dried. There may be gaps in the factual record. Historians must think for themselves and draw conclusions from the historical record that exists.

Though many of the documents used in the above lesson were photographed onsite in the Manuscript Room at the Library of Congress and are not available online, follow-up activities to study the building of the canal in Panama are available. The impact of Roosevelt's persona to sway popular opinion can be seen in the political cartoon *Roosevelt's Rough Diggers*, published as the centerfold in *Puck* magazine, November 14, 1906 (fig. 4.15).

Teachers wishing to develop a lesson on the Panama Canal are encouraged to form small groups to conduct in depth research to address such questions as

- Where is the Panama Canal located? Find a map and compare the two proposed routes.
- Why was the site chosen? What were the political, financial, and geographical considerations? What motivated the players?
- In what ways did the climate and geological challenges present obstacles?
- How were the technological challenges overcome? What did engineers know and need to know about moving large quantities of dirt in Panama's terrain and climate?
- What were the dangers to workers? (In Rick's class, students were impressed by the ultimate success of US engineers to overcome obstacles insurmountable to the French, such as malaria and massive earth slides; see fig. 4.16).

FIGURE 4.16
*Upheaval in Floor of Panama Canal:*
*c[between 1910 and 1914].*
Library of Congress
Prints and Photographs Division.

## STUDENT RESPONSES TO THE PANAMA CANAL DECISION

Students at Thomas Dale High School expressed their evaluation of the Panama decision through an online discussion board. Below are the essential question posed and three sample responses.

**How did the building of the Panama Canal exemplify the best and worst of American vision and decision making?**

Students wrote:

"The Panama Canal was almost the Nicaragua Canal. When France gave up on their construction in Panama, the US saw the potential of the location that had been chosen. This was the shortest route that could be obtained in Central America which would allow for the shortest period of time spent digging. French lobbyists put the good aspects of the area out and forgot to mention all of the reasons that happened to kill much of the work force and forced the project to come to halt. The French just wanted their money back, if they could sell the canal to the US, we would, in effect, pay their debt off that was gained from starting and funding the project. Because we pushed Columbia out through revolution we were made to look somewhat overbearing, but on the flip side we helped not just the world's economy, but also the economy of Central America. Panama, because of this canal, was given large sums of money and now has a world famous trade route running through their tropical country."

"In the story of the building of the Canal I like Roosevelt's quality of determination the most because I really think that is what finally led to achievement of their goal. In general I think determination and enthusiasm like Roosevelt's are the two of the most important qualities when it comes to leading, especially such a big project."

"America was the better choice to build the canal because we had the technological and engineering advances that France did not have. America knew this and took the job because we were trying to be more involved with world interactions. America turned a disease infested hole into a beautiful home for one of the most advanced engineering projects in history."

Source: Katharine Lehman, "Panama Canal Project: Student Online Discussion Board Postings," March 2012.
Thomas Dale High School Library.

## LIST OF PRINT AND ONLINE RESOURCES
## SUPPORTING THE PANAMA CANAL LESSON

Associated Press. "New York World Probes into Panama Canal Scandal, What Became
    of That $40,000,000?" *The Pensacola Journal* (Pensacola, Fla.), 1898–1985,
    December 9, 1908. Image 1—*Chronicling America*. The Library of Congress
    website. http://chroniclingamerica.loc.gov/lccn/sn87062268/1908–12–09/
    ed-1/seq-1.

DuTemple, Lesley A. *The Panama Canal*. Minneapolis, MN: Lerner, 2003.

"Gatun Locks Looking toward Atlantic Entrance of Canal, Showing Tugs, Dredges,
    and Barges Ready for First Lockage from Sea Level up into Lake Gatun . . ."
    Library of Congress Prints and Photographs Division. www.loc.gov/pictures/
    item/96522036.

McCullough, David G. *The Path between the Seas: The Creation of the Panama Canal
    1870–1914*. New York: Simon & Schuster, 1977.

"Panama Canal: A Better Route." *New-York Tribune*. (New York [N.Y.]), 1866–1924,
    January 21, 1902, Page 3. Image 3—*Chronicling America*. The Library of
    Congress website. http://chroniclingamerica.loc.gov/lccn/sn83030214/
    1902–01–21/ed-1/seq-3.

"Panama Canal Construction: Patio of Tenement House Showing Self-closing,
    Fly-proof Garbage Can Stand and Concrete Patio." Library of Congress
    Prints and Photographs Division. www.loc.gov/pictures/item/2004670760.

"The Panama Canal versus the Nicaragua Canal." *The San Francisco Call*. (San Francisco
    [Calif.]), 1895–1913, February 09, 1902. Image 4—*Chronicling America*.
    The Library of Congress website. http://chroniclingamerica.loc.gov/lccn/
    sn85066387/1902–02–09/ed-1/seq-4.

Pennell, Joseph. *Gatun Lock—End of the Day*. Digital image. Library of Congress Prints
    and Photographs Division. www.loc.gov/pictures/item/00649767.

"President Denies Canal Charges." *New-York Tribune*. (New York [N.Y.]), 1866–1924,
    December 16, 1908. Image 1—*Chronicling America*. The Library of Congress
    website. http://chroniclingamerica.loc.gov/lccn/sn83030214/1908–12–16/ed-1/
    seq-1.

*Roosevelt's Rough Diggers*. Digital image. Library of Congress Prints and Photographs
    Division. www.loc.gov/pictures/item/2011645956.

"Stevens and Liquor." *New York Tribune*, July 30, 1905. *Chronicling America*.
    The Library of Congress website. http://chroniclingamerica.loc.gov/lccn/
    sn83030214/1905–07–30/ed-1/seq-14.

*Upheaval in Floor of Panama Canal*. Digital image. Library of Congress Prints and
    Photographs Division. www.loc.gov/pictures/item/det1994019985/PP.

[*U.S.S. Ohio Passing Cucaracha Slide, Panama Canal*]. Digital image. Library of Congress
    Prints and Photographs Division. www.loc.gov/pictures/item/91721892.

Winchester, John. "Nicaragua: No Smoke without Fire." *Stamp Magazine*.
    www.stampmagazine.co.uk/news/article.asp?a=7638.

Discovering for themselves how the Panama Canal decision was made, connecting the dots, and "thinking like historians," students better understood the complexities behind the dry facts in their textbooks. The players became real people. Through open discussion, questioning, and reflection of the primary sources, students remembered the events and outcomes, the trials and triumphs, and President Roosevelt's can-do vision for America.

How can this lesson be applied to decisions being made in Washington today? Students can debate strategies lobbyists use to influence decisions made by Congress. Do we as citizens have better access to information to distinguish truth from fiction than was available in 1902? Can we identify individuals who have vested interests in the outcomes? What is our Panama Canal question today? Thinking like historians, students can apply the lessons of the past to new situations and become wiser citizens.

## CREATING A COMMUNITY OF LEARNING THROUGH WEB 2.0 APPLICATIONS

From a remote location in Colorado, online history teacher Carrie Veatch designs creative and engaging lessons for her students using Web 2.0 applications such as Live Binder, iBooks, and Glogster to involve her students in a community of learning with primary sources. Veatch writes below of her first online project, which began with her research at the Summer Institute.

### World War I Primary Source Propaganda Poster Project

I knew when I came to the Library of Congress for this workshop that I wanted to create a project on World War I because I knew that this was one of the places in my curriculum where we were not analyzing any primary sources. There are propaganda posters in our curriculum, but they are just used a pretty pictures within the text. The students look at them and read captions, but they don't have to do anything with them or analyze them. I had looked at the Library of Congress's digitized collection of World War I propaganda posters before, and I was certain that they could be used to further student understanding, help students make connections, and spark discussion and analysis about topics within our World War I module.

The process of creating my plan began with finding the appropriate propaganda posters. I decided the most logical thing to do was align this assignment with my learning objectives, so I printed out my learning objectives and started sifting through the posters looking for primary sources that fit my mold. I narrowed it down to twelve primary sources that I thought my students could use to prove to me they had met the World War I module's objectives.

I provided twelve primary sources to my students via an online LiveBinder (www .livebinders.com/edit/index/112018) and asked them to select four of those primary sources that would best let them:

- Analyze how and why the US became involved in World War I
- Evaluate the impact of the global war on the US home front
- Identify and judge policy changes enacted in the US as a result of World War I
- Analyze the use of propaganda during World War I and evaluate its consequences and effectiveness

I could see students' understandings grow through this assignment. The primary source propaganda posters really brought our unit of study to life and gave my students the chance to make some amazing connections. I found that my students offered more analysis by recording an audio analysis than they might typically offer in written responses.[17]

As Veatch mentions, one advantage to using the online resources is students' ability to add an audio component to their electronic book to enhance their analysis of the propaganda posters when they create their iBooks (using www.epubbud.com). The final books are posted on the class iBook shelf for everyone to read. Adding the audio component is especially helpful to differentiate learning for students who are more comfortable expressing themselves orally. The transcript of one student's verbal analysis of the "Hun Liberty Bond Poster" (fig. 4.17) illustrates how well she understands the meaning of the poster and confirms Veatch's earlier statement of the connections students made in this unit:

> I think there is a bloody hand to show that the Hun is an insane murderer and he has killed many people. I think this poster was meant to make people want to buy liberty bonds to help free people in Europe from this evil.
>
> Some of my observations were: there is a bloody hand print called "The Hun's Mark" and underneath it says "Blot it out with liberty bonds." This poster is very simple which draws attention to the bloody handprint and the meaning that goes along with it.
>
> Some of my reflections were: to me this poster makes me think that the Hun, like I said earlier, is an insane murderer, which I believe is the intended purpose. I also think that it is meant to indicate that if a person bought a liberty bond they would help stop the murdering.[18]

FIGURE 4.17
*The Hun—His Mark— Blot It Out with Liberty Bonds.* World War I poster by J. Allen St. John. Library of Congress Prints and Photographs Division.

*In this assignment you will be analyzing the use of propaganda posters as media during World War I and connecting content and meaning to your World War I learning objectives.*

# WORLD WAR I PRIMARY SOURCE PROPAGANDA POSTER PROJECT

### Step 1.
View a sample iBook with Mrs. Veatch. View the ePubBud demonstration with Mrs. Veatch. Be sure to schedule a synchronous meeting or watch a recorded session.

### Step 2.
Review the following World War I learning objectives:
- Analyze how and why the US became involved in World War I.
- Evaluate the impact of the global war on the US home front.
- Identify and judge policy changes enacted in the US as a result of World War I.
- Analyze the use of propaganda during World War I and evaluate its consequences and effectiveness.

### Step 3.
You will be creating an iBook that you can share on your mobile device using your www.epubbud .com account. Choose four of the following ten primary source posters from World War I. For each image you will develop an inquiry question related back to your World War I learning objectives.

Then you will create an audio analysis of each poster that includes:
1. An explanation and answer to your inquiry question with connections back to these learning objectives
2. A minimum of three observations
3. Two higher-order questions that you can (research and) answer. (These could be either about the content of the poster or new questions you have about the poster.)
4. Brief reflections on any new understandings
5. At least two cues for iBook readers (e.g., where to zoom) to draw focus to interesting and important pieces of each poster

### Reminders
1. Remember to use the Primary Source Analysis Tool as you examine and analyze each poster and prepare your script.
2. In your ePubBud doc, please format as follows:
   a. At the top of each page type your inquiry question for that poster,
   b. Followed by the embedded poster,
   c. Followed by your embedded audio file,
   d. Followed by a numeric list of your manipulative zoom cues.

### List of World War I Posters Used in the Unit
- No war talk! Attorney General Gregory says, "Obey the law, keep your mouth shut!" http://hdl.loc.gov/loc.pnp/cph.3g09013
- "America, the hope of all who suffer, the dread of all who wrong," Whittier. Save food and defeat frightfulness www.loc.gov/pictures/resource/cph.3g09882

- The Hun—His mark—Blot it out with Liberty Bonds
  http://hdl.loc.gov/loc.pnp/cph.3g09851
- Stand by the boys in the trenches—Mine more coal
  http://hdl.loc.gov/loc.pnp/cph.3g07924
- Chums "When I really began to admire you, my friend, was when you pulled that Lusitania job: When you did that, I said to myself—'There's a man after my own heart!'"
  http://hdl.loc.gov/loc.pnp/cph.3g07819
- The Hun is still watching! Show him we're in earnest—finish the job Victory Liberty Loan
  http://hdl.loc.gov/loc.pnp/cph.3g08129
- Your war savings pledge Our boys make good their pledge—Are you keeping yours?
  http://hdl.loc.gov/loc.pnp/cph.3g08073
- Heroes? past and present
  http://hdl.loc.gov/loc.pnp/cph.3g08060
- If you can't enlist—invest Buy Liberty bonds—See your bank today
  http://hdl.loc.gov/loc.pnp/cph.3g09057
- Save [ . . . ] and serve the cause of freedom
  http://hdl.loc.gov/loc.pnp/cph.3g09740
- Your Liberty Bond will help stop this—Sus bonos de la libertad ayudarán á dar fin con esto
  http://hdl.loc.gov/loc.pnp/cph.3g10652
- Britain is fighting for the freedom of Europe and to defend your mothers, wives, and sisters from the horrors of war. Enlist now
  http://hdl.loc.gov/loc.pnp/cph.3g10902

Source: Carrie Veatch, "World War I Primary Source Propaganda Poster Project: Directions," www.livebinders.com/play/play/112018.

Another online unit Veatch developed for her students had them analyze and compare more than one primary source photograph on a theme using edu.glogster.com. Glogs are online posters that enable students to creatively use sticky notes to write and audio files to dictate their observations, questions, and connections they make regarding the photographs and their knowledge of the topic. See Veatch's assignment, "Primary Source Glogster Assignment."

## PRIMARY SOURCE GLOGSTER ASSIGNMENT

**ASSIGNMENT**

A Primary Source Glogster is a single-page response to a primary source. It is a way to work through the inquiry process and make your own unique understandings of a primary source. It encourages you to think critically and creatively, and it allows you to share your response to a primary source. Through this Glogster, you will ask new questions and construct new ideas; you will also build relationships between the primary source and what you already know about its content.

*Use your http://edu.glogster.com account to create a primary source one-pager glog.*

### Directions

1. Place the primary source image with proper citation in the center of your glog (or link it to the original web page).

2. Write three to four topic sentences and add them to your glog. Be sure it is clear how each idea relates to your understanding of the primary source and adds to the central focus of your glog. Use these sentences as a springboard to explore your own ideas about the primary source.

3. Create clusters around your glog of your dominant observations, reflections, and new questions that you have about the primary source/topic. These clusters could be in the form of text or images.

   – **For OBSERVATIONS: Start each observation with,**
   "I see . . ." Consider the following:
   What do you notice first? Find something small but interesting.
   What do you notice that you didn't expect?
   What do you notice that you can't explain?
   What do you notice that you didn't earlier?

   – **For REFLECTIONS: Start each reflection with,**
   "I think . . ." Consider the following if you get stuck:
   Where do you think this came from?
   Who do you think made this?
   What do you think was happening when this was made?
   Who do you think was the audience for this item?
   Why do you think this item is important?
   If someone made this today, what would be different?
   What can you learn from examining this?

   – **For NEW QUESTIONS: Start with, "I wonder . . ."**
   What do you wonder about . . . Who?
   What?
   When?
   Where?
   Why?
   How?

4. Ask and answer two questions about the primary source. These could be questions that you already know the answer to or questions that you have to investigate.

5. Include at least one new understanding that you have after examining this primary source **OR** a piece of information that you already knew about the topic of this primary source.

6. Conclude your glog with a personal statement about the primary source.

7. Earn extra points by using an audio and/or a video of yourself analyzing this primary source. For example, you could use audio or video for your personal statement.[19]

Source: Carrie Veatch, "Glogster Posters," e-mail message to author, February 6, 2012.

Looking at the glog on women's suffrage (http://mrsveatchthehistoryteach.edu.glogster
.com; fig. 4.18), one can see the student's observations and reflections, which include:

- "I see a woman leaving her babies with a man."
- "I think the man is scared to be left with the babies because he looks very concerned."
- "I wonder how many men were in favor of their wives voting?"

New understandings are presented both in audio recordings and in writing on sticky
notes. In the audio portion, one student comments:

"I chose this photograph (Helena Weed) to compare my political cartoon to because
I thought this was a good example of the opposition the women in the cartoon might face.
First she tries to vote, then she's arrested. Actually I found out that this lady, Helena Hill
Weed was really smart and well educated for her day. She went to a school of mines and
was a geologist. She was arrested in 1917 for protesting for women's suffrage. She was in
jail for 3 days."[20]

On the poster the student quotes the sign Weed was carrying at the time of her arrest,
"governments derive their just powers from the consent of the governed."

After completing the unit, Veatch writes,

I absolutely love this assignment, and more important—so
do my students! This is also one of those assignments that
I can use in just about any history unit that I teach. It has
been my experience that I can use this assignment with
virtually any historical topic and/or primary source.

One student told me that she liked having the option to
record and include her own audio. As an online teacher,
I agree! It is so refreshing to have students submit work in
their own voice, and I really believe that students provide a
more substantial audio analysis than they might in writing.

Another student reflected that creating the Glogster poster helped her organize her analysis more successfully because she is such a visual learner. She told me that having
the primary source in the center of her Glogster poster
and then creating virtual sticky notes, questions, answers,
reflections, and observations helped her pull in more information, ask more questions, and bring her ideas together
more effectively than usual.

I incorporate the Library of Congress' Primary Source
Analysis Tool into this assignment and ask my students to
include down 3–4 observations, reflections, and questions
about their primary source. Since my students work re-
motely online, this helps guide them through the analysis
on their own, and this helps to keep them focused. [21]

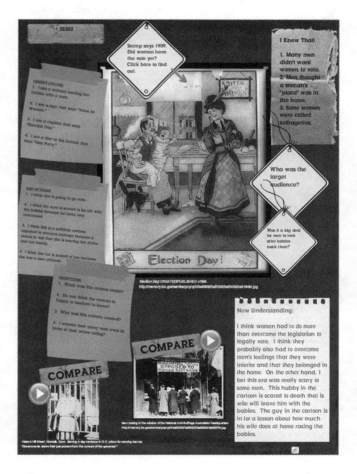

FIGURE 4.18
Screen capture of a student Glogster poster on women's suffrage.

FIGURE 4.19
*Reynolds's Political Map Of The United States, Designed to Exhibit the Comparative Area of the Free and Slave States and the Territory Open to Slavery or Freedom by the Repeal of the Missouri Compromise, 1856.*
William C. Reynolds.
Library of Congress
Geography and Map Division.

## ENGAGING STUDENTS IN LOCAL HISTORY

Our third high school example uses primary sources to draw students into local history. Victoria Abens states that she lives in the unofficial "Underground Railroad capital of the world": Kennett Square, Pennsylvania, where many homes were involved in ferrying fugitive slaves north. Abens is librarian at the Academy of Notre Dame in Villanova, Pennsylvania. Notre Dame is a private, independent Catholic school for girls in grades 6–12.

For this unit she collaborated with the eleventh grade AP (Advanced Placement) United States history teacher to present information on nineteenth-century slavery she located at the Summer Institute. Abens writes:

While at the Primary Sources Institute at the Library of Congress, I began my journey with a simple search for 'slavery' on the Library of Congress—American Memory Internet site. We had completed a lesson on analyzing maps earlier in the day and I thought that might be an interesting route for my lesson. Two maps came up and though similar in a few respects, I was completely intrigued by how different they were. One was a political map of free and slave states from 1850 [fig. 4.19]. It was a beautiful, colorful map with loads of detail and other clarifying information. There was no doubt as to the purpose, creator, and date of this map.

The other map looked to be a pencil sketch and contained absolutely no identifying information. Its bibliographic record merely stated "Underground Railroad." It had the look of something that did not want to be readily identified, and that gave me an idea. If it were a map of stops on the Underground Railroad, what would it mean if it were found in someone's possession? What would it mean to the abolitionists whose homes provided protection? These questions gave rise to even more concerning the secrecy of the Underground Railroad. How could this intricate network of people and places remain so secretive? How were the lines of communication conducted among and between slaves and abolitionists? What role did illiteracy of the slaves play, if any? My hope was to help the students get into the minds of the slaves and the abolitionists. What was it really like to be an escaped slave on the run? What was it like to be an abolitionist and put yourself and family at such great risk for a cause you believe in? My hook to reel the students in was to remind them that participating in the Underground Railroad was illegal but to consider what role morality played in the minds of the abolitionists. Was there anything to compare this to today? I took this assignment one step further by assigning each student to locate and review a slave narrative, also provided on the Library of Congress site under the Federal Writer's Project. The narratives are catalogued several different ways and I found that searching them by "Location" involved the most streamlined search. This really helped [students] see the point of view of the slave and assess their very different stories and reasons for escape.

The final project was initially to write a first person reflection paper from either the point of view of an escaped slave or of an abolitionist aiding an escaped slave. The classroom teacher decided to change this to include a few more perspectives and instead of a reflection paper, assigned the students to a role-play. Therefore, the final assignment was to work in groups and, using excerpts from several primary sources, including slave narratives, role play a position as either a southern planter, slave, abolitionist, democrat, or northern slave catcher.[22]

The final assignment can be viewed on Vicki Abens's Wikispaces pathfinder page, http://ndaundergroundrailroad.wikispaces.com. The essential question given students at the beginning of the unit is: "How did the Underground Railroad, which involved so many people, remain secret?" As they compare the two maps, students are guided by the teacher to:

- Observe and identify details in two different historic maps
- Understand and reflect on the reasons for the differences
- Apply this understanding to the secrecy and success of the Underground Railroad

To hook students into connecting the issues surrounding the Underground Railroad to their lives today, they debate understanding morality versus legality. They address important questions such as:

- Is it ever okay to break the law?
- Can you think of an instance today where that would be okay?

After using the Primary Source Analysis Tool (fig. 2.17) to record their observations, reflections, and questions for each map, students write a one-page reflection on the differences they find while analyzing the maps to explain the role these differences play in the secrecy and success of the Underground Railroad.

Abens explains on the wiki that students are guided in their questioning during the activity period to encourage a focus on the detail, clarity, purpose, creator, and quality of the maps. Students are reminded to reflect on their observations, which leads to deeper thinking and questioning.

**Questions of import:**

- How did slaves acquire knowledge of the Underground Railroad and its inherent risks and dangers?
- How were the lines of communication between and among abolitionists and slaves conducted and controlled?
- What impact, if any, did the illiteracy of the slaves have on the Underground Railroad?
- Who else was at risk in this process besides the slaves?
- Why would slaves risk so much to make this journey (introduction of personal narratives and 1st person thinking)?[23]

---

### MATERIALS USED IN THE UNDERGROUND RAILROAD UNIT

Wikispaces pathfinder for the unit including the lesson plan, the PowerPoint presentation, materials, images, and guiding questions designed by Vicki Abens
- http://ndaundergroundrailroad.wikispaces.com

Reynolds's political map of the United States, designed to exhibit the comparative area of the free and slave states and the territory open to slavery or freedom by the repeal of the Missouri Compromise. Library of Congress Geography and Map Division.
- www.loc.gov/resource/g3701e.ct000604/seq-1

Underground railroad map of the United States, ca. 1838–1860.
Federal Writer's Project. Library of Congress Geography and Map Division.
- www.loc.gov/resource/g3701e.ct001517/seq-1

Primary Sources Analysis Tool
- www.loc.gov/teachers/usingprimarysources/resources/Primary_Source_Analysis_Tool.pdf
- www.loc.gov/teachers/usingprimarysources/resources/Analyzing_Maps.pdf

---

FIGURE 4.20
Students at San Rafael High School analyze photographs of migrant workers to present their "Interview a Portrait" assignment to their class. Photograph by Esther Kligman-Frey.

## "MIND WALKWING" INTO HISTORY WITH SFMOMA

Our final example showcases a unique moveable classroom inspired by ArtThink, an online curriculum site, created by the San Francisco Museum of Modern Art. Esther Kligman-Frey, a teacher trainer for SFMOMA, carries her lesson to classrooms in the San Francisco Bay community. She opens students' eyes to other times and places first by guiding them to understand primary sources using the Mind Walk activity. Students fill out the activity worksheet to trace the evidence of their lives in a twenty-four-hour period (fig. 4.20).[24]

"The students commented that in this digital age, there are a lot less examples of trace evidence on paper," Kligman-Frey states. "They came up with new examples: security camera at school, ATM cameras, twitter, Facebook, text messages, voice mail, and e-mail. One student commented: 'I have had some experience with primary sources, but only in a scholarly context. It was eye opening to apply the concept to my life.'"[25]

Once students understand the concept of primary sources, Kligman-Fry introduces photographs from historical collections at the Library of Congress and has students pair up to "interview" a portrait such as Dorothea Lange's *Migrant Mother*. See "SFMOMA's 'Interview a Portrait' Lesson" for Kligman-Frey's description of the experience.

## SFMOMA'S "INTERVIEW A PORTRAIT" LESSON

The "Interview a Portrait" lesson is part of a thematic group of lessons taken from the SFMOMA ArtThink website. The specific theme is "Portraiture: Revealing Ourselves and Others." The description from the teacher's guide is: "Artists have always been interested in capturing likenesses of themselves and other people. Successful, complex portraits reveal not only what the sitter looks like, but also aspects of his or her character, and even something about the attitudes of the artist. Dorothea Lange was a photographer whose images captured the joys, sorrows, poverty, and prosperity of Americans in the first half of the 20th Century."

The "Interview a Portrait" lesson was presented in May 2012 to a senior English class. All the books the class read during the school year were about "the individual." "Interviewing a Portrait" fit right in with their task of delving into the characters. We discussed the power of a photograph. Each ArtThink lesson has a big-idea question; for this lesson, the question was: "What can a portrait tell you about a person?" Some other essential questions we discussed were:

- How do photographers construct stories using visual means?
- What are some of the stories Lange tells through her photographs?
- How do her photos elicit sympathy for her subjects?

FIGURE 4.21
*Migrant Mother*, 1936.
Photograph by
Dorothea Lange.
Library of Congress
Prints and
Photographs Division.

Projecting the photograph *Migrant Mother* (fig. 4.21) from the Library of Congress Prints and Photographs Division and describing the photograph analysis activity, the students filled out the activity sheet, and we analyzed the photograph together. What students wrote on the Primary Source Analysis Tool sheet:

- **Observe**—Family looks poor, clothes dirty and ripped, mother looks old and wrinkled, no father, two children hiding, mother holding a baby, she looks tired, sad and depressed, living in a tent
- **Reflect**—Mother is thinking about how she is going to feed her kids, shows what people are going through, shows how hard times were, brings light to squalor in the '30s, a father missing, the govt. needed to help people who lost their jobs
- **Question**—Where's the father? Where are you from? Is there any other support for your kids? What is your daily life like? Why are you so sad? Why are your kids looking away? What do you see for the future?
- **Further Investigation**—Where is the Migrant Mother now? What happened to her kids? What are her kids doing today?

**The students were then given the "Interview a Portrait" assignment:**
Pair up with a classmate and select a portrait whose subject you would like to interview. With your partner, using the activity tool analyze the photograph you have chosen and write questions to ask the person in the picture.

- **For example:** Where were you born? Where did you study? Where did you work? What kind of life did you lead?
- **Research the time period**—the Depression—and specifically the migrant workers in California.
- **Analyze the photograph you chose.** One of you should ask the questions and write down the responses while the other answers as if he or she were the person in the portrait. You will present your interviews to the class.

Students were shown how to get to the Dorothea Lange pages of photographs taken of the migrant worker in California during the Depression: from the Library of Congress home page, click on "Prints and Photograph Collection," scroll to "Farm Security Administration," then type *Dorothea Lange, Migrant* and click "Go"; thumbnails of an array of Lange's photos appear on the page.

Sources: "Interview a Portrait: Introduction," SFMOMA ArtThink, accessed June 16, 2012, www.sfmoma.org/artthink/lessonintro.asp?lessonid=50; Esther Kligman-Frey, e-mail message to author, June 14, 2012.

As students summarized their reflections of the Lange photographs, their comments provide evidence that they learned to experience the Depression firsthand through Dorothea Lange's lens, not reconstituted from a secondary description in a textbook. The people and times became real. Students wrote:

"Lange infuses her photographic subjects with a quiet, dignified struggle."

"Her photographs showed real emotion, not just a pose. You can actually feel what is going on in the picture. You can see the pain of the people, back in the day."

"Her photos made America seem like a 3rd World country. I learned how depressing it was during the depression."[26]

Kligman-Frey has gone on to repeat this lesson in other classrooms with other photographs from the Library of Congress digital collections. She writes: "I also presented this lesson—'Interview a Portrait'—to two history classes. The students were studying the '20s. I used a photograph from the Library of Congress of Babe Ruth for the "Analyze a Photograph" activity. Then, they chose their portrait to analyze and interview from a number of subjects from the '20s, such as Langston Hughes, Babe Ruth, Al Capone, Tut Jackson, Al Jolson, Charles Lindbergh, flappers and prohibition. By doing this same lesson on a different subject area, I have gained confidence that the 'Interview a Portrait' lesson works very well."[27]

---

### MATERIALS USED IN THE "INTERVIEW A PORTRAIT" LESSON

**Sources from the Library of Congress**

**Mind Walk Activity**
- www.loc.gov/teachers/professionaldevelopment/selfdirected/introduction/PDF/MindWalkActivity.pdf

**Primary Source Analysis Tool**
- www.loc.gov/teachers/usingprimarysources/resources/Primary_Source_Analysis_Tool.pdf

**Teacher's Guide—Analyzing Photographs and Prints**
- www.loc.gov/teachers/usingprimarysources/resources/Analyzing_Photographs_and_Prints.pdf

**Sources from the San Francisco Museum of Modern Art**

**ArtThink website**
- www.sfmoma.org/artthink

**Interview a Portrait—Introductory > Language Arts > Portraiture: Revealing Ourselves and Others**
- www.sfmoma.org/artthink/lessonintro.asp?lessonid=50&lessoncategoryid=2&menu=i

**Dorothea Lange—Introductory > History/Social Studies > A Documentary Passion**
- www.sfmoma.org/artthink/lessonintro.asp?lessonid=43&lessoncategoryid=3&menu=i

---

## SUMMARY

The lessons in this chapter are included to provide the reader with examples of strategies used to successfully engage students in high-quality learning experiences to interact with history through primary sources. Designed by individuals inspired by their weeklong Summer Institute experience, these lessons are classroom tested. When added to lessons described in chapter 2 prepared under the direction of the Library of Congress Educational Outreach team (www.loc.gov/teachers/classroommaterials/lessons) and the lessons described in chapter 3 created through the professional development module training, these lessons provide strategies and examples to support classroom teachers seeking to locate, modify, and design lessons to meet their specific curriculum needs. Once teachers and students begin to uncover the wealth of images and artifacts available through the Library of Congress collections, the learning opportunities and connections to local curriculum and interests grow and grow.

## NOTES

1. Teresa St. Angelo, "Using Primary Sources in Kindergarten," e-mail message to author, April 9, 2012.

2. Ibid.

3. Ibid.

4. Jennifer Burgin, "Primary Sources Project Plan Outline: Teaching with Primary Sources." Library of Congress Summer Institute, Summer 2011, 3.

5. Jennifer Burgin, "Explorers and Maps Lesson Plan," e-mail message to author, May 1, 2012.

6. Ibid.

7. Sandy Rodeheaver, "Washington Crossing the Allegheny Lesson," e-mail message to author, January 4, 2012.

8. Sandy Rodeheaver, "Primary Source Project Plan: Outline. Teaching with Primary Sources," Library of Congress. May 26, 2011, 1–4.

9. Sandy Rodeheaver, "Washington Crossing the Allegheny Lesson," e-mail message to author, May 23, 2012.

10. "Summer Reading 2011," Garrett County Summer Reading Program, accessed May 24, 2012, http://cardinal.ga.k12.md.us/Summer2011/Home.html.

11. Rodeheaver, "Washington Crossing the Allegheny Lesson."

12. Abigail Housen and Philip Yenawine. "Visual Thinking Strategies: Understanding the Basics," accessed September 12, 2012, www.vtshome.org/research/articles-other-readings.

13. Ron Ritchhart and David Perkins, "Making Thinking Visible," *Educational Leadership* 65, no. 5 (February 2008): 60.

14. Krista McKim, student work samples, "Primary Source Project", e-mail message to author, July 21, 2012.

15. Sam Wineburg, "Thinking Like a Historian," *Teaching with Primary Sources Quarterly* 3, no. 1 (Winter 2010): 2–4, www.loc.gov/teachers/tps/quarterly/historical_thinking/pdf/historical_thinking.pdf.

16. David G. McCullough, *The Path between the Seas: The Creation of the Panama Canal 1870–1914* (New York: Simon & Schuster, 1977), 291.

17. Carrie Veatch, "Online Experiences," e-mail message to author, June 1, 2012.

18. Transcript of student voice recorded on iBook describing The Hun poster.

19. Veatch, "Online Experiences."

20. "Suffrage," Glogster.Poster_yourself, audio transcript accompanying Helena Weed photograph, accessed June 20, 2012, http://mrsveatchthehistoryteach.edu.glogster.com/suffrage.

21. Veatch, "Online Experiences."

22. Victoria Abens. "Underground Railroad," e-mail message to author, November 29, 2011.

23. Victoria Abens, "Academy of Notre Dame, 11th Grade-United States History, 19th Century Slavery, Underground Railroad," accessed November 29, 2011, http://ndaundergroundrailroad.wikispaces.com.

24. "Mind Walk Activity," worksheet, Library of Congress, www.loc.gov/teachers/professionaldevelopment/selfdirected/introduction/PDF/MindWalkActivity.pdf.

25. Esther Kligman-Frey, "Interview with a Portrait Lesson," e-mail message to author, June 14, 2012.

26. Ibid.

27. Ibid.

## BIBLIOGRAPHY

Abens, Victoria. *Underground Railroad.* http://ndaundergroundrailroad.wikispaces.com.

Bain News Service. *French Officers Watering Horses.* Digital image. Library of Congress Prints and Photographs Division. www.loc.gov/pictures/item/ggb2005017385.

*Baum, Geo. L., Captain, 11/18/19.* Digital image. Library of Congress Prints and Photographs Division. Accessed May 16, 2012. www.loc.gov/pictures/item/npc2007000768.

Blaeu, Willem Janszoon. *Nova Totius Terrarum Orbis Geographica Ac Hydrographica Tabula [1606].* Digital image. Library of Congress-American Memory Map Collection. http://memory .loc.gov/cgibin/query/h?ammem/gmd:@field(NUMBER+@band(g3200+ct001217v)).

Canot, Pierre Charles, *The Indians Delivering Up the English Captives to Colonel Bouquet.* Digital image. Library of Congress Prints and Photographs Division. www.loc.gov/pictures/ item/2003666448.

*Farm Security Administration/Office of War Information Black-and-White Negatives—Background and Scope—Prints & Photographs Online Catalog (Library of Congress).* Library of Congress Home. www.loc.gov/pictures/collection/fsa/background.html.

Fly, C. S. *[The Captive White Boy, Santiago McKinn in Geronimo's Camp, with Group of Indians, Mostly Children, in Front of Partially Constructed Tent, before Geronimo's Surrender to Gen. Crook, March 27, 1886].* Digital image. Library of Congress Prints and Photographs Division. www.loc.gov/pictures/item/2006682475.

Housen, Abigail, and Philip Yenawine. "Visual Thinking Strategies: Understanding the Basics." *Visual Understanding in Education.* www.vtshome.org/research/articles-other-readings.

"Interview a Portrait: Introduction." SFMOMA ArtThink. www.sfmoma.org/artthink/lessonintro .asp?lessonid=50.

"The Journals of George Washington & Christopher Gist: Mission to Fort Le Boeuf." The Old Stone House Museum. September 29, 2009. http://oldstonehousepa.org/2009/09/29/ now-available-the-journals-of-george-washington-christopher-gist-mission-to-fort -le-boeuf.

Lange, Dorothea. *Migrant Mother: Destitute Pea Pickers in California. Mother of Seven Children. Age Thirty-two. Nipomo, California.* Digital image. Library of Congress Prints and Photographs Division. www.loc.gov/pictures/resource/fsa.8b29516.

Library of Congress. "Mind Walk Activity: Teaching with Primary Sources, Chapter 2." www.loc.gov/teachers/professionaldevelopment/selfdirected/introduction/PDF/ MindWalkActivity.pdf.

McCullough, David G. *The Path between the Seas: The Creation of the Panama Canal 1870–1914.* New York: Simon & Schuster, 1977.

McKim, Krista. "Primary Source Project Plan: Outline. Teaching with Primary Sources." Library of Congress Summer Institute, 2011.

Mills, Charles E. *Franklin's Experiment with the Kite, 1911.* Digital image. Library of Congress Prints and Photographs Division. www.loc.gov/pictures/resource/cph.3b42841.

"Primary Source Analysis Tool." PDF. Teacher's Guides and Analysis Tool—Library of Congress. www.loc.gov/teachers/usingprimarysources/resources/Primary_Source_Analysis_Tool .pdf.

Rakeman, Carl. 1753—*Washington Crossing the Allegheny.* Digital image. Federal Highway Administration; US Department of Transportation. September 14, 2011. www.fhwa.dot .gov/rakeman/1753.htm.

Reynolds, William C. *Reynolds's Political Map of the United States, Designed to Exhibit the Comparative Area of the Free and Slave States and the Territory Open to Slavery or Freedom by the Repeal of the Missouri Compromise.* Digital image. Library of Congress Geography and Maps Division. www.loc.gov/item/2003627003.

Ritchhart, Ron, and David Perkins. "Making Thinking Visible." *Educational Leadership* 65, no. 5 (February 2008): 57–61.

Rodeheaver, Sandy. *Primary Source Project Plan: Outline. Teaching with Primary Sources.* May 26, 2011. Library of Congress, Washington, DC.

*"Roosevelt's Rough Diggers Illus. In: Puck, v. 60, No. 1550 (1906 November 14)*, Centerfold." Digital image. Library of Congress Prints and Photographs Division. www.loc.gov/pictures/item/2011645956.

St. John, James Allen. *The Hun—His Mark—Blot It out with Liberty Bonds, 1917 Poster.* Digital image. Library of Congress Prints and Photographs Division. 2012. www.loc.gov/pictures/item/2002722433.

"Summer Reading 2011." Garrett County Summer Reading Program. http://cardinal.ga.k12.md.us/Summer2011/Home.html.

"Telegram from Philippe Bunau-Varilla Papers, 1877–1955." Cromwell to P. Bunau-Varilla. June 26, 1902. Library of Congress Manuscripts Division, Washington, DC.

*Upheaval in Floor of Panama Canal:c[between 1910 and 1914.* Digital image. Library of Congress Prints and Photographs Division. www.loc.gov/pictures/item/det1994019985/PP.

Underground Railroad Map of the United States, ca. 1838–1860. Library of Congress-American Memory Map Collection. www.loc.gov/item/75696205.

US Supreme Court Justices, 1973. Digital image. Library of Congress Prints and Photographs Division. www.loc.gov/item/75696205.

Vetch, Carrie. "World War I Propaganda Posters—LiveBinder." World War I Propaganda Posters—LiveBinder. www.livebinders.com/play/play/112018.

Waldseemüller, Martin. *A Map of the Entire World According to the Traditional Method of Ptolemy and Corrected with Other Lands of Amerigo Vespucci, 1507.* Digital image. World Digital Library Hosted by the Library of Congress. www.wdl.org/en/item/369/zoom.

Wineburg, Sam. "Thinking Like a Historian." *Teaching with Primary Sources Quarterly,* (Winter 2010): 2–4.

# Discovering Local History Resources in Your Own Backyard

MARY ALICE ANDERSON

A special memory of teaching fourth-grade students is seeing them enthusiastically look at school scrapbooks and yearbooks housed in the computer lab. The students excitedly viewed old photos, school records, and newspaper clippings. They laughed at the clothes their teachers wore twenty years ago, connected with family names they recognized, and were curious about the handwritten school attendance log. It was the perfect follow-up to an instructional activity based on examining digital primary source photographs. The students were engaged and eager to touch and see these local history treasures.

## LOCAL HISTORY RESOURCES ARE ALL AROUND US

Local history documents are the documents, photographs, and artifacts we study in city, county, and neighborhood museums. They are historical menus hung on walls or displayed in shadow boxes at local restaurants. They are artifacts displayed in lobbies of local businesses, hospitals, and universities. Local history resources are created every day with the publication of birth or marriage announcements, obituaries, interviews, and news stories in local newspapers. These resources help tell the stories of our communities, neighborhoods, and families. Local history resources often tell a very geographically and culturally unique story. For example, The Polish Cultural Institute in Winona, Minnesota (www.polishmuseumwinona.org), reflects the distinct heritage of the Kashubian Polish who settled in Winona and western Wisconsin. Other local history museums and collections share stories that have a broader impact. The Greyhound Bus Museum in Hibbing, Minnesota, conveys the history of a bus system originally established to provide transportation for workers from nearby towns who worked in open pit ore mines at Hibbing. The museum also depicts Greyhound's impact on transportation and industries across the country (www.ironrange.org/attractions/historic/greyhound). Museums, collections,

FIGURE 5.1
*Sugar Shack, Sacopee Valley, Maine. 2009.*
Photograph by Ivy Demos.

FIGURE 5.2
*Young Neighbor (Julia Fletcher) of Frank H. Shurtleff*
*Gathering from Sugar Trees for Making Maple Syrup.*
Photograph by Marion Post Wolcott. *America and the Great Depression:*
*Photographs from the FSA-OWI, 1935–1945, American Memory Collection.*
Library of Congress.

and displays such as these document a wide range of the human experience right in our own backyards.

## LOCAL HISTORY PERSONALIZES THE PAST AND MAKES IT COME ALIVE

Studying local history makes the past more relevant as students learn about their community's past, customs, and culture—the who, what, when, where, and why become more tangible and real. Knowledge of local history helps provide a sense of place and builds a sense of pride in a community's uniqueness. Personal knowledge helps build future community citizens and leaders. Backyard resources help students become more thoughtful searchers of information because they often bring prior knowledge and personal experience to the process.

A Wisconsin teacher used newspaper archives to help students connect their lives to their city's past: "The closing of the local GM plant in 2008 sent the local newspaper into a reflection mode. At the same time, students were studying the Great Depression. Newspaper interviews with long-time autoworkers' remembrances of Janesville's GM history were a terrific resource to help students share and record their experiences as this transition to life after GM is underway. These oral interviews are powerful primary sources."[1]

Studying local history is "doing history." A Maine educator spent a weekend playing tourist in her own Sacopee Valley visiting family-run and neighbor-supported maple syrup shacks (fig. 5.1). She was moved by the experience of meeting her students in their comfort zone. The event showed how kids were making connections with their community: "They were openly bragging about the setups they would have in their future."[2] She photographed the process, artifacts, and even newspaper clippings to share her experiences with students at a school-wide Maple Syrup Day she planned. "Last year I used my photos to have the kids make a timeline of maple syrup technology. The kids loved it and teachers noticed."[3] She also discovered a 1940 photo in the Library of Congress that depicts a young woman making maple syrup (fig. 5.2). The photo complemented her own photos that she shared at her school's Maple Syrup Day.

## WHERE CAN I FIND RESOURCES LIKE THESE FOR MY STUDENTS? HOW CAN I USE THEM?

This chapter addresses how to find digital local history resources in the *American Memory Collections*, selected other Library of Congress divisions, and your own community. We will also learn how educators can find and use local history resources to engage and motivate students as they study local history.

## DOES AMERICAN MEMORY COLLECTIONS HAVE SOMETHING ABOUT MY BACKYARD?

First-time users of the *American Memory Collections* are often surprised to discover artifacts about their local community or neighborhood, especially if it is not a large city. Often they expect the collections to only have resources about major events and places in American history; it's quite the opposite! *American Memory Collections* have digital artifacts representing neighborhoods and communities of all sizes, expanding the accessibility of local history resources far beyond what is available locally.

**Take a break from reading for a fun first search:**

1. Log in to http://memory.loc.gov.
2. Enter your community's name and state in "Search All Collections."
3. Use "Gallery View" to see an overview of your results (fig. 5.3).
4. Select the item you want to view or hear.

Quite likely you will find a photo, map, historic film, document, or interview with a local resident. An Iowa high school teacher librarian was excited by her nine hits from three collections, including *Panoramic Photographs FSA/OWI* (http://memory.loc.gov/ammem/collections/panoramic_photo), when she searched for pictures of her small rural community. "I even found a picture of the [high school] in 1913 [and] a picture of the main four corners in 1908. After analyzing it with my husband we recognized some of the buildings that are still standing!"[4]

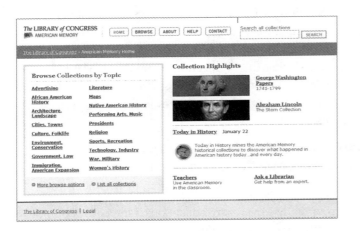

FIGURE 5.3
Screen capture of a gallery view from the *American Memory Collection* refined by "Format: Photo, Print, Drawing"; "Location: State"; and "Location: city."

**FIGURE 5.4**
*Interior View, Basement, Looking Southwest at the Gear Pit Below the Grinding Stones, Showing Wooden Cogs Attached to Underground Turbines. Friction Drive Visible behind Control Bar (left) Which Operates Smut Mill, Schech's Mill, Beaver Creek State Park, La Crescent, Houston County, MN.*
Library of Congress Prints and Photographs Division.

If your city is large, narrow your search to your neighborhood or a familiar landmark. A Brooklyn, New York, teacher realized her students knew very little about their neighborhood or borough. She discovered turning them loose with their own searching was highly motivational. If your city or general location is not listed, broaden your search using a county or region name. For example, there are no photos or maps of the city of Houston, Minnesota, in the collections, but there are twenty-three photos and drawings of a rural Houston gristmill in the collection *Built in America: Historic American Buildings Survey/Historic American Engineering Record/Historic American Landscapes Survey, 1933–Present* (http://memory.loc.gov/ammem/collectionshabs_haer; fig. 5.4).

A fun first search like this motivates students of all ages. Young researchers have fun finding something familiar or something new and are eager to share their discoveries.

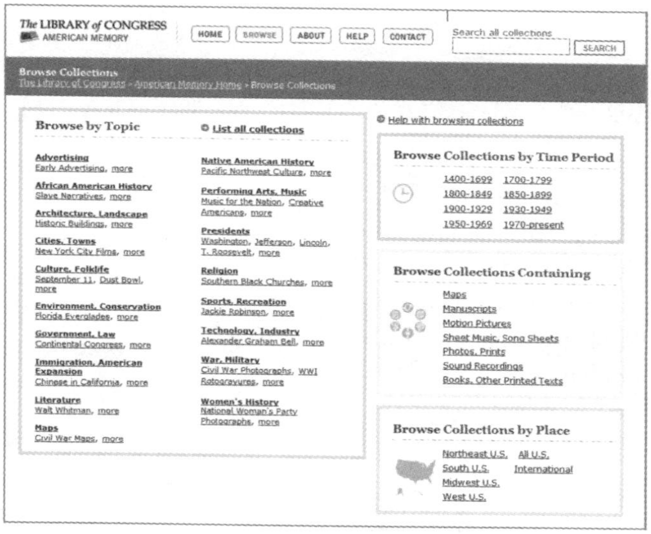

## WHAT'S NEXT?
## WHAT OTHER WAYS CAN I SEARCH?

If you know what you are searching for and have the correct words or phrases to use, go ahead. If not—or even if you do—take the time to browse. Browsing is an interesting and productive way to discover local history treasures including some you may not have even thought of. Serendipitously discovered resources sometimes turn out to be the best. The "Browse Collections" page (fig. 5.5) offers many choices and makes browsing easy. First, take the time to browse "Collections by Place." It groups collections in five geographic regions: Northeast US, South US, Midwest US, West US, and US International collections. As an example, selecting Northeast region yields nine million items in sixteen collections.

**FIGURE 5.5**
Screen capture of the Library of Congress *American Memory* page "Browse Collections by Place."

Next, look at selected collections using the "Collections Containing Maps" browse method and at others in the "Collections Containing Photos, Prints" group. These are effective starting places to locate local history primary sources in formats especially appealing to a wide range of students.

1. Select "More Browse Options" on the *American Memory* home page.
2. Select "Collections Containing Maps" or select "Collections Photos, Prints."
3. Browse the list of collections paying attention to geographic pertinence.

The "Photos and Prints" grouping has over sixty collections. One collection not to be missed is *Built in America: Historic American Buildings Survey/Historic American Engineering Record/Historic American Landscapes Survey, 1933–Present* (www.loc.gov/pictures/

collection/hh). It is a unique collection that can be browsed by subjects and geographic regions. HABS/HAER/HAL has an extensive assortment of engineering, architectural, and landscape drawings. The geographic search makes browsing easy by state, county, and city or town when you are unsure of which search terms to use. Teachers can use these resources to implement interdisciplinary local history lessons with subjects such as art, drafting, or physics.

### Panoramic Photographs: Taking the Long View, 1851–1991 from the Detroit Publishing Company
http://memory.loc.gov/ammem/collections/panoramic_photo

Search the collection of over four thousand photos using the place index, or use a keyword search to search within the collection. Students will like these oversized photos on topics such as natural disasters and cities. They might recognize a photo from a reproduction on display in a local museums or city building.

### Panoramic Maps, 1847–1929
http://memory.loc.gov/ammem/pmhtml/panhome.html

FIGURE 5.6
*Bird's-eye View of Canon City, Colorado, County Seat of Fremont County 1882* from "Panoramic Maps, 1847–1929."

Bird's-eye drawings show streets, buildings, and the terrain in the forty-eight continental United States and four Canadian provinces. Search by location name or use the state geographic index with subject headings for locations and cities. Some maps have building and location guides. Maps are colorized or sepia. Zoom in to see details of a street and compare what you see in the historical image to now. "What's changed?" discussions are a natural and easy approach to integrating these maps into the study of local history. A third-grade teacher used one prior to taking her class on a historic walking tour of her city's downtown. Ask your students to compare their city's map to a neighboring city's. What's the same? What's different? (See fig. 5.6.)

### Railroad Maps, 1828–1900
http://memory.loc.gov/ammem/gmdhtml/rrhtml/rrhome.html

These maps show the development of transportation, industry, and agriculture via the US railroad. A geographic index guides the searcher to 683 maps in regions of the United States and individual states. A detailed geographic location index includes maps "that are narrowly focused on a geophysical or cultural feature such as a water body, mountain, county, city, or battlefield." Use "Gallery View" to easily identify the type of map.

### Civil War Maps
http://memory.loc.gov/ammem/collections/civil_war_maps

### Utah and Western Migration Collection
http://memory.loc.gov/ammem/award99/upbhtml/overhome.html

These distinctive collections have both local history and general curriculum connections. Students in Perryville, Kentucky, could search "Civil War Maps" by place to find a map about the Battle of Perryville. What can maps of Midwest states or territories tell us about the war in that part of the country? Students in western states could search the migration collection by trail name to find a historical map of their area. The collection includes some interactive maps to better help students understand the materials. Photos, diaries, and letters add to the appeal and usefulness for students anywhere.

### Even More Maps! Maps and Cartographic Items: 1500–Present
http://memory.loc.gov/ammem/gmdhtml/gmdhome.html

This comprehensive collection of collections should not be overlooked. A geographic index is useful for finding maps representing cities and towns, conservation and environment, discovery and exploration, cultural landscapes, transportation, military battles, and campaigns. There are also guides to places in the news and places in history. Teams of students could search specified map categories to locate what's available in relation to their backyard.

## MANUSCRIPTS

Use the browse option "Collections Containing" to search "Manuscript collections." Many of these collections are geographic specific. Browse through the collections title list for names of collections pertaining to your locale. Manuscript collections also include non-text digital resources. Some unique examples with a specific geographic focus suitable for studying local history and culture are described below. These three manuscript collections all have applications beyond the geographic focus and local history.

- **The Chinese in California, 1850–1925**
  http://memory.loc.gov/ammem/award99/cubhtml/cichome.html
  This collection documents Chinese immigration through diverse primary resources including letters, business records, pamphlets, broadsides, and political cartoons. A senior high teacher was excited about using authentic Chinese language documents to make connections with a non-English-speaking Chinese immigrant student. The collection helps students learn understand situations that immigrant groups of all types have confronted throughout our history.
- **The African American Experience in Ohio, 1859–1920**
  http://memory.loc.gov/ammem/award97/ohshtml/aaeohome.html
  Manuscripts here range from personal letters of an African American soldier to manumission papers (the minutes book of an antislavery group) and slavery remembrances. Search by keyword or browse through format categories including newspapers.
- **Prairie Settlement Nebraska Photographs and Family Letters**
  http://memory.loc.gov/ammem/award98/nbhihtml/pshome.html
  The letters from the family of a homesteader discuss land, work, neighbors, crops, religious meetings, and problems with grasshoppers, financial problems, and the Easter Blizzard of 1873.

## SOUND RECORDINGS

Browsing sound recordings is another way to discover local history surprises that make history come alive. Each collection is different; however, audio files are available in multiple formats, and transcripts, text, and photos are usually part of the collection. Two collections are described below; watch for more information about *Folk Fiddle Music, Southern Appalachian, and The Henry Reed Collection Multi-format—1966–1967* later in the American Folklife Center section of this chapter.

- *Working in Paterson, Occupational Heritage in an Urban Setting*
  http://memory.loc.gov/ammem/collections/paterson
  This contemporary collection of over four hundred oral interviews was created in 1994. There is a detailed place index and extensive photographs help show how history happens every day. Maps and essays provide additional historical context. The Paterson materials are a project of the American Folklife Center.

- *American English Dialect Recordings*
  http://memory.loc.gov/ammem/collections/linguistics
  The Center for American Linguistics has recordings of the voices and dialects from 33 states and some Canadian provinces. Speakers represent rural and urban locations, famous people, and ordinary citizens. The collection is searchable by name, place, title, or subject.

These examples are intended as starters to illustrate how the vast *American Memory* collections can be used to find specific information about your community. Another option is browsing the subject headings to expand your list of possibilities within any collection. No matter which approach you take or which collection you search in more depth, take time to learn how the collection is organized and what tools will help you focus on local history. Dig deep; expect the unexpected!

## BEYOND THE *AMERICAN MEMORY* COLLECTIONS: DISCOVERING LOCAL HISTORY RESOURCES THROUGHOUT THE LIBRARY OF CONGRESS

As you know from earlier chapters and references, the *American Memory* collection represents just one of the library's home page features and one route to finding resources for your classroom. In this section we'll look at selected Library of Congress resources that will help you engage your students in the study of local history.

- *The Sanborn Fire Insurance Maps*
  www.loc.gov/rr/geogmap/sanborn
  This database is a searchable group of fire insurance maps from 1881 stored in the Library of Congress Map Division Reading Room. Over five thousand of these large and unique maps representing over half of the fifty states, Canada, and Mexico are online for everyone to view. Search the collection by country, state, building type, or keyword. Use the "Sanborn Samplers" (www.loc.gov/rr/geogmap/sanborn/san4a2.html) to see examples of how paring fire insurance maps with panoramic maps provides a glimpse into community history.

FIGURE 5.7
Screen capture of *Chronicling America, Historic American Newspapers* from the Library of Congress website.

- *Chronicling America,*
  *Historic American Newspapers*
  http://chroniclingamerica.loc.gov
  This portal (fig. 5.7) gives access to information in historic newspapers. Students can search over five hundred historic newspapers pages from 1836–1922. Newspapers represent large cities and rural areas in twenty-five states and the District of Columbia. A topic list includes topics widely covered in the press when the paper was published. A drop-down menu to search by state is helpful because many newspapers have changed names, merged

with others, or been discontinued. Results can also be filtered by year. Advanced searching provides options for searching selected newspapers. The "All Digitalized Newspapers" option allows searching by state, as well as selected ethnicities and languages. The "U.S. Newspaper Directory, 1690–Present" has more than 140,000 newspapers and additional searching filters to locate newspapers available through a variety of state and local entities. These newspapers are fun, exciting, and educational. Use them for the popular "Today in history" or "What happened on my birthday?" activities.

## THE AMERICAN FOLKLIFE CENTER

This previously mentioned resource (www.loc.gov/folklife) uniquely preserves the everyday lives of individuals, communities, and regions. It helps us understand that songs, language, games, personal stories, everyday life, and community roots are local history, too. The center's "Guide to Online Collections and Presentations" (www.loc.gov/folklife/onlinecollections.html) is very helpful. One section highlights several *American Memory* online collections and may lead you to resources you may not have previously considered. Examples are:

- *Florida Folklife from the WPA Collections, 1937–1942*
  http://memory.loc.gov/ammem/collections/florida
  Features folksongs and folktales in many languages as well as interviews and life histories.
- *Fiddle Tunes of the Old Frontier: The Henry Reed Collection*
  http://memory.loc.gov/ammem/collections/reed
  Documents music and history of Virginia's Appalachian region.
- *Quilts and Quiltmaking in America*
  http://memory.loc.gov/ammem/qlthtml/qlthome.html
  Features photographs and recorded interviews with six quilt makers in Appalachian North Carolina and Virginia (fig. 5.8).

These collections broaden our understanding of local history and culture and offer diverse interdisciplinary teaching opportunities. Math students, for example, could identify geometric shapes in quilts while art students can study colors and design their own quilts.

**FIGURE 5.8**
Screen capture of *Cathedral Window* quilt, detail. From the American Folklife Center, Library of Congress, Blue Ridge Parkway Folklife Project Collection.

The Folklife Center's *Local Legacies* (www.loc.gov/folklife/roots) celebrates the cultural heritage and uniqueness of each state and territory by documenting the arts, crafts, and customs of traditional community life. Selected festivals, parades, and local observations of local and national holidays are featured. The collection is searchable and text is understandable to young learners. Students can browse for information by selecting a state map, state name from a list, or entering a key word. Students in Michigan, for example, could use *Local Legacies* to learn about Michigan's National Baby Food Festival, Hamtramck Polish Day, or the Blossomtime Festival. Members of Congress contributed to *Local Legacies*.

*Folklife Resources for Educators* (www.loc.gov/folklife/teachers/index.html) emphasizes "place-based and community-based teaching materials" and is a portal for searching by curriculum area, grade level, state, or resource type. Educators can find lesson plans, websites, and teaching tools available through entities such as Smithsonian museums, arts organizations, and state education agencies.

*Folklife in Your State* (www.loc.gov/folklife/states/index.html) is a guide to Library of Congress digital collections and to materials accessible only in Library of Congress Reading Rooms. The state-by-state guide also highlights resources specific to the District of Columbia and United States trust territories. Use the guide as one more avenue to discovery.

The American Folklife Center's resources should not be missed; the resources will add a new dimension to the study of local history engaging students with their own community's culture and heritage.

## THERE'S MORE!
## OTHER GUIDES FOR FINDING LOCAL HISTORY RESOURCES

- *State Digital Resources: Memory Projects, Online Encyclopedias, Historical & Cultural Materials Collections*
  www.loc.gov/rr/program/bib/statememory
  This collection identifies digital collections created by state, county, and local entities. These are not resources created or maintained by the Library of Congress, but are conveniently accessible through the portal. Indiana students, for example, can search *Indiana Memory*, *Indiana Historical Society Images*, and *Indiana Digital Archives* for artifacts such as wills or military records. *Iowa Pathways* from Iowa Public Television has a wealth of primary sources and lesson ideas. A Minnesota middle school student couldn't locate a historic picture of a local landmark; her grandmother who works at the public library showed her how to search *Minnesota Reflections*, the state's memory project. The student was thrilled. Educators will want to take time to learn the intricacies of their state's collections.
- *State Resource Guides*
  www.loc.gov/rr/program/bib/states
  These guides compile digital materials available throughout the Library of Congress website. In addition, each guide provides links to external websites and a bibliography of selected works for both general and younger readers. The guides are a work in progress and also include resources from territories and Washington, DC.

## THE TEACHERS PAGE AS A PATHWAY TO LOCAL HISTORY RESOURCES

The Library of Congress teacher's guide is described extensively in chapter 2. Two especially helpful "Teachers" page resources are "Search by Standards" (fig. 5.9; www.loc.gov/teachers/standards/index.php) and "Primary Sources by State."

### SEARCH BY STANDARDS

Use the drop-down menu to search state standards by grade while selecting from three subjects: language arts, social studies, and library/technology.

- *Library of Congress Primary Sources by State*
  www.loc.gov/teachers/classroommaterials/primarysourcesets/states
  Select your state on the "Primary Sources by State" map to view thumbnail images of representative Library of Congress primary resources associated with your state. US territories and the District of Columbia are also represented. When browsing from the "Teachers" page, click on "Classroom Materials, Primary Source Sets" and scroll down to "Primary sources by state."

FIGURE 5.9
Screen capture of "Search by Standards" from the "Teachers" page of the Library of Congress website.

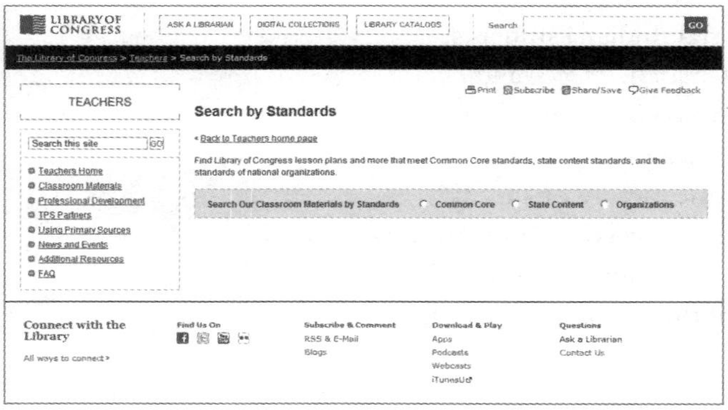

The compact representation is a convenient starting place for educators just starting to use the Library of Congress and also an easy starting place for students. A "Teachers" page blog post by Sara Suiter and Anne Savage from July 14, 2011, has local history teaching ideas stemming from the clickable map mentioned above (http://blogs.loc.gov/teachers/2011/07/primary-sources-by-state-making-local-connections).

Up to now this chapter has discussed a rationale for studying local history, highlighted curriculum activities, and suggested how to find local history resources available through the Library of Congress. In the remaining sections we will look at local history resources in your own community, education standards addressing the study of local history, and curriculum examples from teachers and school librarians.

## LOCAL HISTORY RESOURCES: OFTEN IN THE LEAST EXPECTED PLACES

> I have not used many local resources in teaching social studies. I wasn't aware what was available. When I begin teach history again, I absolutely plan on visiting the local history museum.
> —*Bryan DesLauriers, rural Vermont teacher, St. Albans, Vermont, spring 2011*

The perfect resources are sometimes hard to find because they are off the beaten path or because we simply overlook what is right in front of us. We won't know what's right in our own backyard or online unless we take the time to explore, ask questions, and learn. Be a tourist in your own community or neighborhood. Think about where you would take visitors. A New York educator did both and said, "It's incredible what I've learned about my neighborhood!"

Start with the obvious—often a county or city museum. The museum may be fully staffed in an easily accessible building. Or, local resources may be housed in an old church, school, or railroad depot staffed by volunteers and only open a few days a month. Either way, the people who work there will be more than willing to help you and will be happy you thought of them. In 2011 I made my first visit to a 150-year-old historic gristmill less than ten miles from my home (fig. 5.10). I was totally amazed by the extent of the six-story mill's collection of equipment and artifacts. During the Civil War the mill shipped flour down the Mississippi River for the Union troops. The mill office is full of record books and historic newspapers. The dedicated volunteers who passionately maintain the historic site were very eager to tell me about their special collection of old photographs. The website has photos, historical information, and movies of equipment in operation. (Visit Historic Pickwick Mill online at http://pickwickmill.org.)

FIGURE 5.10
*Historic Pickwick Mill Flour Dresser*, Pickwick, Winona County, Minnesota. July 15, 2011. Photograph by Mary Alice Anderson.

## JUMP-START YOUR THINKING WITH SOME MINNESOTA EXAMPLES

Here are a few examples from smaller Minnesota cities to jump-start your thinking about what you might discover in your city or neighborhood. Winona, a Southeast Minnesota city of 28,000, is home to the Winona County History Center, a large and active society with permanent and visiting exhibits. The archives have photos, clippings, newspapers, telephone books, census information, and staff to assist daily visitors. Society websites provide access to digitized information. *A Civil War Journal, Minnesota's Company K, Company K, Minnesota, 1st Volunteer Infantry Regiment at Gettysburg, July 1–14, 1863*, is a collection of local Civil War journals, photos, diaries, newspaper articles and letters including several written by the real-life Charley Goddard, the young soldier in Gary Paulsen's young adult novel *A Soldier's Heart* (www2.smumn.edu/deptpages/~history/civil_war/index.htm). City newspapers from the 1800s through the late twentieth century are available digitally through a project with the state university.[5]

Corporate museums also portray the city's past. The Watkins Company Museum houses photographs, advertisements, cookbooks, spice tins, and documents. A miniature town with well-known landmarks and buildings is a children's favorite. The corporate website has photos, company history, and a timeline (www.jrwatkins.com/timeline).

Other southeast Minnesota examples are the Minnesota State Orphanage in Owatonna (www.orphanagemuseum.com), where visitors can relive thousands of personal stories about a unique chapter of Minnesota history, and Austin's Spam Museum (www.spam.com/spam-101/the-spam-museum). Visitors have fun learning about a local company with a large local economic impact, its best-known products, and Spam's important role in World War II.

## CITY AND NEIGHBORHOOD MUSEUMS

Many cities, large and small, have their own museums. The Milwaukee Public Museum with its popular displays of historic Milwaukee streets is one example (www.mpm.edu). The museum was one stop on the Doors Open Milwaukee Weekend in 2011. The event was an opportunity to experience the city's architectural environment in a way like never before. Participants were invited to discover over one hundred great buildings that are integral to Milwaukee's history, economy, and culture, both past and present, and see the inner workings of notable locations throughout the metro area.[6]

Milwaukee's Bay View neighborhood has an abundance of historic sites and active historical society. (Later in this chapter we will see how Bay View students help make Bay View's history come alive.) A house in the Minneapolis suburb of Richfield, Minnesota, was preserved to help tell the history of a first-ring suburb. Its story was showcased by Mary Jane Smetanka in the *Star Tribune*.[7] The National Hellenic Museum in Chicago (www.nationalhellenicmuseum.org) chronicles the Greek American journey through exhibitions and oral history. There are also exhibits on ancient Greece.

Very small towns have museums, too. Rollingstone, Minnesota, has a museum celebrating the town's Luxembourg heritage. Community members actively maintain ties with Luxembourg and preserve the history. The entire small town of Mineral Point, Wisconsin, is on the National Register of Historic Places. Buildings and museums reflect the contributions of Cornish miners (http://mineralpoint.com/history).

What are unique treasures are in your community? Start looking. It's fun.

## HISTORY OFF THE BEATEN PATH

Signatures, a Winona restaurant, displays old postcards in plexiglass frames as table centerpieces. They trigger conversations about the recipient and sender. Local artifacts from restaurants, manufacturers, and educational institutions are displayed in shadow boxes. A Vermont teacher discovered local history artifacts as he was leaving the local hospital after the birth of his child!

> As I was leaving the hospital I noticed an area just off the lobby that displayed a small collection of primary sources. It includes about two-dozen photographs from the 1920s through the 1950s, a lithograph of Saint Albans in 1877 and an original of the warranty deed given to build the first hospital from 1883. I realized that this really is a small exhibit/collection of local primary sources that could be used in a student field trip and/or digitized, analyzed by local students, and linked to both the hospital and museum's websites.
> —Bryan DesLauriers, *"Online Course Postings: Teaching with Primary Sources,"* comment, *rural Vermont teacher, St. Albans, Vermont, March 28, 2011*

You never know where you will find something of interest. Consider these other possibilities for locating physical and virtual resources.

- **National museums located in your community.** The museum's mission might be to preserve the story of a significant national event, such as World War II, but will likely have a section dedicated to the local community.

- **Specialty museums or private collections.** These are often developed by an individual to preserve artifacts of unique interest.
- **Colleges and university archives or museums.** Knowledgeable staff at institutes of higher education often partner with other educators to promote access to information and promote historic preservation.
- **Public libraries.** Staff often maintain local history sections that include city directories, phone books, and other records. Locally or self-published books or pamphlets will be helpful.
- **City halls and county courthouses.** These government buildings provide innumerable primary source local history documents. Visit both to learn about the availability of public records, including online records.
- **Cemeteries, cemetery records, and cemetery websites.** These are rich in community history.
- **Memorials, statues, historical plaques, and other markers.** These markers alone may have enough information to tell a story. Businesses and homes of significance often have plaques with historical background.
- **People!** Employees and volunteers at tourism bureaus, convention centers, and visitor centers are there to promote the community. They are a wealth of knowledge and can direct you to other people to help you.
- **Public radio and television.** Programming archives feature stories (and thus history) told through video and audio.

Online directories of museums are another starting place to locate additional information:

- **The Association of American Museums**
  www.aam-us.org/about-museums
  A professional association representing museums and museum staff.
- **Museumlink's Museum of Museums**
  www.museumlink.com
  Lists museums by state.
- **American Local History Network**
  www.alhn.org
  Makes digital resources accessible by state and topic. The focus is "independent, genealogical and historical websites."

## BECOME FAMILIAR WITH STANDARDS AND GUIDELINES

Local history is addressed in national standards. *The National Curriculum Standards for Social Studies* explain the significance that an understanding of local and community history, culture, and human interactions has in the development of social studies literacies, critical thinking, and civic engagement at all grade levels.[8] The *Common Core State Standards Initiative* project integrates reading standards for literacy in history with social studies 6–12 and specifically addresses using primary sources. For example, students in grades 6–8 will "determine the central ideas of information of a primary or secondary source; provide an accurate summary of the source distinct from prior knowledge or opinions."[9] Relating the use of primary sources to topics students connect with and understand will foster a desire to dig for more information.

The National Center for History in the Schools identifies broad topics and supporting standards for grades K–4 (www.nchs.ucla.edu/Standards/standards-for-grades-k-4). Topics are: "Living and Working Together in Families and Communities, Now and Long Ago," and "The History of Students' Own State or Region." State standards typically address local history in elementary school. By studying their neighborhood and community, students can make connections between their community and regional, state, and national history. New York standards, for example, address local history in several grades in the New York Social Studies Core Curriculum (www.p12.nysed.gov/ciai/socst/pub/sscore1.pdf). Fourth-grade teachers are encouraged to consider themes such as local Native American tribes and the period of industrial growth and development in New York State. The standards suggest that "students can investigate local events and issues and connect them to national events and issues."[10] Students in grades 7 and 8 are expected to "use local resources to examine the role of your community in the Civil War and local attitudes toward it."[11]

Learn about your state standards, local curriculum, and units of study to help your students succeed. Don't be surprised if local history projects become students' favorite projects.

## ADVOCATE AND PUBLICIZE

Websites, blogs, Twitter accounts, Facebook pages, and newsletters are all good advocacy tools. Blogs are relatively easy to create and maintain, making them a natural choice for telling others about those exciting local resources and treasures that are often ignored because they are too close to home. The often informal nature of a blog makes it easy to write directly to students and teachers. Public library and museum blogs about local history resources and activities are prolific. Why leave this task to others? Local history and culture websites draw attention to online and physical resources that may be otherwise difficult to find. One media specialist's local history page has a link to the local winter carnival and highlights to the longest running event of its type in the US. Be sure to include links to pertinent resources on the Library of Congress collections as well. Locally created and maintained online resources and those available to us through state and national organizations may be overlooked if educators do not point them out! Online links help give students more time to use and interact with the information in meaningful ways.

## CREATE PARTNERSHIPS

Museums and higher education library staff are natural partners. Both want students to visit their facilities, to discover what they offer, and to learn how to do inquiry-based historical research. Teachers can learn what's accessible on campuses and possibly forge partnerships and arrange to bring the kids on campus to explore. Museums and universities often have guides available for K–12 teachers and students. An intern at the Winona County History Center developed a guide correlating museum resources and activities with elementary standards in writing, reading, language, and literacy. Guides could easily be replicated by a team of educators and museum staff. The collaboration will benefit everyone. The Winona County History Curriculum shown in table 5.1 was developed by the Winona County History Center in 2011 (www.winonahistory.org). This section points out resources teachers can use when students study the county's Luxembourg heritage.

## BRING MUSEUM RESOURCES TO THE SCHOOL

Education coordinators bring artifacts and speakers to classrooms and media centers. Education trunks are a favorite among many educators and a great resource if funds or limited time make a field trip to the museum impossible. The Winona Middle School media specialist partnered with the Winona County History Center to establish ongoing, rotating displays of museum artifacts in the media center (www.hermantown.k12.mn.us/ high/Library_Archives). Students especially enjoyed a display of all toys; parents liked a "going to school long ago" display. Other funds were used to pay for digitizing, printing, and framing historical photographs for display in the media center, and purchasing historic preservation supplies to help preserve old newspapers.

The school media specialist also partnered with a historian in 1999 to develop a website, Wabasha Prairie to Winona, on Winona's early history (www.winonahistory.org/ sesqui) and with teachers to develop a website on Winona's ethnic groups. The latter is recognized under the section "Learning: Engage and Empower" of the US Department of Education's 2010 *Transforming American Education: Learning Powered by Technology* (www.ed.gov/technology/netp-2010) as an example of collaboration and leveraging simple technology so that it can be locally sustained and maintained.[12] Both projects were funded through local and regional grants.

---

### HOSPITAL-TEACHER PARTNERSHIP

The Vermont teacher quoted above did not forget the artifacts he discovered in the hospital. He continues:

*I returned days later with a pad of paper and a camera and went straight to the receptionist to introduce myself. She was busy so I began taking pictures and notes. This is where I learned something about hospital protocol. She noticed I was taking pictures and called the head of public relations that came down to question what I was doing. I explained my task and this course and we had a 20–30 minute conversation about the pictures and about possible plans in the future to have students analyze and digitize their entire collection (many more pictures are available but not currently displayed). She thought that a partnership like this would be fantastic and she even emailed me a brief history of the hospitals in Saint Albans. All in all, I'm glad that I looked suspicious as it worked in my favor . . . I can easily foresee having my students complete a project like this with the hospital and other places in the community such as a local restaurant in particular would be housed on the local historical society's website.*

—Bryan DesLauriers, "Online Course Postings: Teaching with Primary Sources," comment, rural Vermont teacher, St. Albans, Vermont, March 28, 2011

Table 5.1. Lessons and corresponding K–6 writing standards.

| LESSON TITLE | ACTIVITIES | READING STANDARD |
| --- | --- | --- |
| Farming in Winona County | Where Does Your Garden Grow? | N/A |
| | Little House on the Prairie, The Woods and the River | N/A |
| Mississippi River Trunk | History Talks | 7. Conduct short as well as more sustained research projects based on focused questions, demonstrating understanding of the subject under investigation. |
| | | 8. Gather relevant information from multiple print and digital sources, assess the credibility and accuracy of each source, and integrate the information while avoiding plagiarism. |
| | | 9. Draw evidence from literary or informational texts to support analysis, reflection, and research. |
| | Cause and Effect (with cards) | N/A |
| | From Lazy River to Deep Water | N/A |
| | Which Way Is North? | N/A |
| Pioneers Trunk | Miscellaneous worksheets | 9. Draw evidence from literary or informational texts to support analysis, reflection, and research. |
| | Readings, pictures, object exploration | 1. Write arguments to support claims in an analysis of substantive topics or texts, using valid reasoning and relevant and sufficient evidence. |
| | | 3. Write narratives and other creative texts to develop real or imagined experiences or events using effective technique, well-chosen details, and well-structured event sequences. |
| Luxembourg Immigration Curriculum (Part of Pioneers Trunk) | Where Did We Come From? | N/A |
| | World Traveler: Using an Atlas | 3. Write narratives and other creative texts to develop real or imagined experiences or events using effective technique, well-chosen details, and well-structured event sequences. |
| | | 4. Produce clear and coherent writing in which the development, organization, and style are appropriate to task, purpose, and audience. |
| | Delicious Country | N/A |
| | Holland, Luxembourg, Belgium Video Visits | N/A |
| | Eat Your Country | N/A |
| | Luxembourg Day (Stations) | 9. Draw evidence from literary or informational texts to support analysis, reflection, and research. |
| | Where I Live / Journal of Children of the World | 3. Write narratives and other creative texts to develop real or imagined experiences or events using effective technique, well-chosen details, and well-structured event sequences. |

Source: Winona County Historical Society, *Winona County Historical Society Activities: Learning Luggage Series*, 9, www.winonahistory.org/wordpress/wp-content/uploads/Winona-County-History-Curriculum1.pdf.

## PRACTICE HISTORIC PRESERVATION
## IN THE SCHOOL MEDIA CENTER

Create a history room. Library staff in the northern Minnesota community of Hermantown started a history room and project of community value when they established a physical and digital archive of school history and activities (fig. 5.11; www.hermantown .k12.mn.us/high/Library_Archives). They started with a yearbook collection and then invited community members to contribute school memorabilia, including such items as newspaper clippings, diplomas, scrapbooks, and videos. A local club comprised of people who had lived in a Depression-era housing project donated its funds and scrapbooks to the library media center. The funds were money to start a Minnesota books collection that that has books about townships. Previously one of the organizers, Bob Silverness, worked with students at Proctor High School to develop "Passion, Pride, Tradition. . . . Legacy" booklets celebrating the school's golden anniversary.[13]

> Knowing what happened within the walls of your school or in your street or in your neighborhood is a connection between the kids and big picture. . . . One Halloween, for fun, I told my juniors ghost stories from the White House. This led to them telling me stories about their homes. One girl was completely convinced her house was haunted. Crazy lead in, but after our discussion, she became really interested in the history of her house in the Garden District of New Orleans and started researching the house, the area and eventually started doing work with a local preservation group. That is satisfying!
> —Robin Vogt, "Online Course Postings: Teaching with Primary Sources," comment, schoolteacher at Isidore Newman School, New Orleans, Louisiana, August 5, 2011

FIGURE 5.11
Screen capture of "Hermantown Archives," Hermantown Community Schools.

Start small when an ambitious project like Hermantown's is not possible. Creating a yearbook collection, even at the elementary level, is good place to start. Former graduates or city residents often visit our city's senior high school library to search yearbooks. Archive yearbooks and catalog them in the online catalog so that searchers can find out what yearbooks are available before they arrive. If the catalog isn't public, post the list on the school's website. Offer to start displaying school artifacts in the library. Kids of all ages will love the involvement and interacting with school artifacts. Consider digitally archiving portions of the school's websites that depict significant events in the school's history so they are available to future researchers. The National Archives has an idea-packed web page, "Establishing a School Archives," to help you get started (www.archives.gov/about/history/building-an-archives/school-archives.html). Celebrate your school's history!

## MORE EXAMPLES FROM THE FIELD

Several curriculum ideas are spread throughout this chapter. We learned how a Wisconsin teacher used historic newspapers to help students connect their current circumstances with the Great Depression and how a Maine school librarian paired the local tradition of collecting maple syrup with *American Memory* resources to increase student understanding of local customs. These successful projects were expanded after their initial success. Steve Strieker, the Wisconsin teacher, continued making student and curriculum connections between the Great Depression of the 1930s and the early twenty-first century local economy. Students used Library of Congress newspapers and photos to research the Great Depression and publish their own *Great Depression Gazette* articles using a class Google site. Personal reflections about how the current economic fallout impacted them, their families, and friends are posted anonymously on a class Google blog. "My dad went to school," "Both parents lost jobs," "Living paycheck to paycheck," "Everlasting Recession," and "Friend died" were representative of over seventy deeply felt reflections.[14]

In this chapter's final section we will look at more actual curriculum ideas and other possibilities for helping students connect with local history.

Stephanie Stocks, the Iowa high school teacher librarian who was excited about the panoramic photos she found of her rural Iowa county in the *American Memory* collections, was inspired to search for local history resources close to home. She visited the nearby Backbone State Park, which has many buildings built by the Civilian Conservation Corps. The park is also home to the Iowa Civilian Conservation Corps Museum. Stocks planned a student field trip so students could learn more about the work of the corps in Iowa. Students were asked to record interesting discoveries and photograph or videotape the evidence of the CCC work remaining at the park. She uploaded digital images and photos to Voice Thread; students described the images and shared that their lives are still impacted by the work of the CCC. Students also read transcripts of oral interviews with former corps members from the area.[15] To learn more about the corps in Iowa, visit these sites:

- **The CCC Legacy Website** (look under CCC History Center/CCC Museums) www.ccclegacy.org
- **Backbone State Park** (look under Destinations/Iowa's State Parks) www.iowadnr.gov
- **Iowa's oral history project** (look under Destinations/State Parks & rec Areas/ Civilian Conservation Corps/ CCC Interviews & Photos) www.iowadnr.gov

Students at the Winona Area Learning Center worked with an artist in residence to design and paint a mural representing their city's past and future. The students wanted the mural to represent what their community means to them. They liked it personally because it's not just historical. It is what they think of Winona; not what people think they will see.[16] The mural depicts the geography, environment, new and old buildings, and local color. Their group art class project hangs in the school's lobby. A writer for the *Winona Post* interviewed the students about local elements in the mural and explained the details for the Artists in Residency program that made the project possible.[17]

## SHARING COMMUNITY PRIDE

Student-created print, video, or audio walking stories are one way to engage students with local history and foster community pride. Bay View High, Wisconsin, students produced an audio walking tour of Bay View that highlights historic landmarks. The twelve episodes were created in partnership with the Milwaukee Observatory project and made available on the observatory's website (fig. 5.12; www.milwaukeeobservatory.com/archaeology/walkingtours). Student knowledge and pride in their community is evident.

The website and tour are part of larger collaborative projects between Bay View Schools, the Bay View Historical Society, and the Milwaukee Public Museum.

> The purpose of the collaboration is to create a stronger sense of belonging in the Bay View community. As society changes, families move, and the economy challenges the stability of neighborhoods, BVHS knows that working together for the good of everyone will build relationships, offer support, and create resources that are vital for growth, connection and future development. The community-building project will offer students, staff, families, businesses, neighbors, historical society members and elders in Bay View time to learn and participate together. We continue to encourage a sense of community by conserving, celebrating and sharing Bay View's rich heritage.[18]

Museum staff and educators are slowly building the infrastructure for learning history with more students in the future. Teachers and third-grade students created a trifold flyer with photos and text highlighting significant historical buildings in their small rural community. They also placed the information on their school's website.

All you need for you and your students to replicate these projects are basic word processing or desktop publishing tools and a free, easy-to-use audio recording tool such as Audacity. These Bay View students also learned about their community through geocaching activities. Geocaching supported a classroom goal of using the town as a resource and learning more about their community's history through the discovery of caches in the town and a nearby state park.

FIGURE 5.12
Screen capture of the Bay View walking tour web page, www.milwaukeeobservatory.com/walkingtours/bayview.

Monica McQuaid's Glogster poster gives students an enticing introduction to Georgia Agirama, Georgia's official museum of agriculture and life on a nineteenth-century farm (fig. 5.13). Photos, a map, and a video invite students on a virtual tour before they attend heritage workshops. Students take their own photos at Agirama and create their own Glogster posters. The photo project is enhanced with a written reflection of their experiences at Agirama, what they learned, and what they would have missed from today's life if they lived in the 1880s.

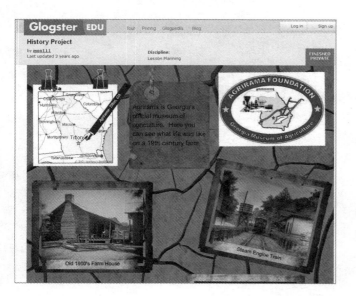

## A TEACHABLE MOMENT

After students visited the National Eagle Center in Wabasha, Minnesota (www.nationaleaglecenter.org), I followed up with a short activity. We talked about why Southeast Minnesota is home to the National Eagle Center and examined the 1832 *Eagle Map of the United States* (fig. 5.14). In this unique map Florida becomes the eagle's claw, Maine his beak. Students found Southeast Minnesota in his wing. Teachers across the river in Wisconsin could make a local connection with the "Old Abe the Battle Eagle" song (fig. 5.15).[19]

FIGURE 5.13 (Top)
Screen capture of "History Project" highlighting Agrirama: Georgia's Official Museum of Agriculture, http://mon111.edu.glogster .com/history-project/. Monica McQuaid, teacher.

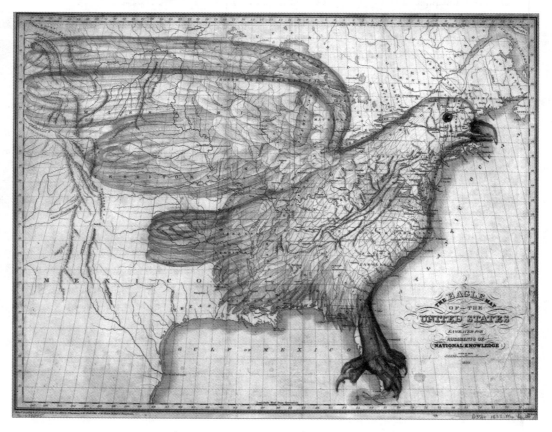

FIGURE 5.14 (Right)
*The Eagle Map of the United States / Engraved for Rudiments of National Knowledge, 1832.* Isaac W. Moore, Library of Congress Geography and Map Division

## CONNECTING KIDS AND FAMILY HISTORY

A personal favorite memory for me is working with a sixth-grade teacher when her students completed a family timeline project. Students interviewed a family member about his or her life and used local history resources to find more information about significant local "historical" events the family member shared. They created timelines overlapping key events in the family member's life with contemporary local history events. Students presented their timelines and shared a personal family artifact that told a story during a project showcase. One student proudly shared her grandmother's ticket to a 1957 Elvis concert, one brought in his grandfather's World War II navy uniform, and another displayed a toy tractor as he described his family's farm heritage.

Today we could integrate a variety of twenty-first century Web 2.0 tools in a similar project. A few options are:

- Conduct online interviews with family members in diverse locations and keep a transcript of each session using Web 2.0 software such as Today's Meet.
- Record family stories using Audacity or another audio recording tool to accurately record the interview.
- Generate timelines using a web-based tool. Layers are a unique feature that make it easy to show events going on at the same time. Preceden is free, but registration is required.
- Share stories through safe social media discussion boards or blogs such as Edmodo. Students can share their stories and Preceden timeline links safely using student-friendly online tools.
- Post a historic community photo; invite family members to record and share their remembrances of a place or event through software tools such as Voice Thread.
- Collect family objects and use them as a catalyst for multigenerational family discussions and story sharing. See ideas found in "History in Household Objects," an EDSITEment lesson (http://edsitement.neh.gov). One activity encourages students to get together with a parent or grandparent to talk about 1950s-era objects depicted on the website and how they were used. Objects from earlier and later time periods are also included.

FIGURE 5.15
Sheet music title page for "Old Abe the Battle Eagle," song and chorus poetry by L. J. Bates, esq.; music by T. Martin Towne, author of *Our Boys Are Coming Home*, 1865, Library of Congress, Rare Book and Special Collections Division.

## THEN-AND-NOW ACTIVITIES:
## MATCHING LOCAL HISTORY WITH INQUIRY

New Orleans teacher Robin Vogt connected personally with a photo of boat pilot stepping onto the dock at Pilottown, a small community that serves as a location for Mississippi River pilots to guide ships across the sandbar and up and down the river. Vogt wrote, "The photo was great to find it as it reflects an important part of my husband's family history. It evokes the scent of creosote and diesel fuel that was Pilottown before it was destroyed almost completely by Hurricane Katrina in 2005."[20] Further inspired by photos taken after Hurricane Katrina, she planned "The Disappearance of Pilottown," a classroom photo analysis activity comparing contemporary photos with photos taken in 1938 (figs. 5.16 and 5.17).

FIGURE 5.16 (Right)
*Pilot Stepping from Boat to Dock, Pilottown Louisiana.* Photograph by Russell Lee. From *America from Great Depression to WWII, FSA/OWI 1935–45,* Library of Congress.

FIGURE 5.17 (Bottom)
*Selected Panoramic Photos: A City Two Months Old: Nome City, Alaska.* Panoramic photographs. Library of Congress.

For help getting started with a then-and-now activity, consider the Library of Congress collection *Seeing Change Over Time* (www.loc.gov/collection/panoramic-photographs/articles-and-essays/selected-panoramic-photographs), which features photos from Duluth, Minnesota; Nome, Alaska; and Boston, Massachusetts, as well as information about the history of selected panoramic photos.

Or, use the Atlanta Time Machine website with its extensive collection of then-and-now photos in several categories including downtown, homes, and businesses (www.atlantatimemachine.com).

- Then-and-Now Activity IdeasCreate a digital or printed display of then-and-now photos depicting buildings or geographic locations. Students of any age can search for and view historical photos before taking their own photos for a photo essay.
- Enhance a Google map of a historic neighbor or city with historic photos.
- Use Adobe Photoshop to create a photo overlay of historic photos with current photos made transparent.
- Use augmented reality tools such as such as History Pin to create a past/present photo archive.

When students use technology tools such as these in combination with local history resources they are no longer just viewing, reading, or listening—they are interacting with each other in new ways and creating new resources. They are engaged in learning and applying and expanding critical thinking.

As explained in chapter 2 and previous sections of this chapter, the "Teachers" page is jam-packed with ideas. Two features not to be missed are "The Branding of America" and "Explore the States" because the brief, easy-to-read text will appeal to elementary and middle school students. "The Branding of America" features a clickable map and links to iconic brands from a majority of the states (www.loc.gov/teachers/classroommaterials/presentationsandactivities/presentations/branding; fig. 5.18). For example, the Georgia link provides information about Coca-Cola; while Greyhound buses, mentioned earlier in this chapter, represent Minnesota. Teaching ideas and resource links are included. Use "The Branding of America" activity as a springboard for creating student-produced product maps about their community or region.

"Explore the States," an *America's Library* feature, provides basic state information and resource links to photos, music, and multimedia accessible through a clickable map (www.americaslibrary.gov/es/index.php). Milwaukee, Wisconsin, students will have fun reading about their city's annual circus parade or Harley-Davidson, one of the city's best-known industries. Hibbing, Minnesota, students can learn about Greyhound buses. Teachers everywhere can use the map under "Explore the States" to help students get thinking about what they would include on their own map.

FIGURE 5.18
Screen capture of "The Branding of America—For Teachers" from the Library of Congress website.

## SUMMARY

It's often said that all history is local. Whether your history is found in the millions of resources available through the Library of Congress, in the archives of your county's museum, or in your own school, it can be a resource for investigation, further understanding, and developing community pride. As you can see from this chapter's description of the various tangible and digital content many teachers have used, local history resources are everywhere. Once you learn what's available, you will have a treasure chest of ideas to engage students.

## NOTES

1. Steven Strieker, "Online Course Postings, Teaching with Primary Sources," comment, University of Wisconsin–Stout, March 21, 2010, https://uwstout.courses.wisconsin.edu/d2l/home.

2. Ivy Demos, "Online Course Postings, Teaching with Primary Sources," comment, University of Wisconsin–Stout, March 22, 2009, https://uwstout.courses.wisconsin.edu/d2l/home; Demos, e-mail message to author, October 30, 2011.

3. Ibid.

4. Stephanie Stocks, "Online Course Postings, Teaching with Primary Sources," comment, University of Wisconsin–Stout, March 21, 2010, https://uwstout.courses.wisconsin.edu/d2l/home.

5. "Winona Newspaper Project Presented by the Winona State University Darrell W. Krueger Library," Winona State University website, accessed March 31, 2012, www.winona.edu/library/databases/winonanewspaperproject.htm.

6. Kathleen Dunn, "Doors Open Milwaukee Weekend," *The Kathleen Dunn Show*, WPR Ideas Network, Wisconsin Public Radio, Program 110922E, September 22, 2011, http://wpr.org/search/ideas_program_search.cfm?StartRow=1&startyear=1&keyword=doors+open+milwaukee&x=13&y=9.

7. Mary Jane Smetanka, "A State Full of History and People to Tell It," *Star Tribune* (Minneapolis), December 10, 2010, www.startribune.com/local/west/111704679.html.

8. "The National Curriculum Standards for Social Studies: A Framework for Teaching Learning and Assessment," *NCSS Bulletin* 111 (2010).

9. "Reading Standards for Literacy in History/Social Studies 6–12," *Common Core State Standards for English Language Arts & Literacy in History/Social Studies, Science, and Technical Subjects*, 61, www.corestandards.org/assets/CCSSI_ELA%20Standards.pdf.

10. New York State Department of Education, *Social Studies Core Curriculum*, 9, accessed July 23, 2013, www.p12.nysed.gov/ciai/socst/pub/sscore1.pdf.

11. Ibid., 19.

12. US Department of Education, *National Education Technology Plan 2010: Learning: Engage and Empower*, accessed April 1, 2012, www.ed.gov/technology/netp-2010.

13. Marie Kelsey, "Saving School and Community History: The Hermantown High School Archival Project," *Minnesota Media* (2003): 34–36, accessed March 31, 2012, www.hermantown.k12.mn.us/high/Library_Archives; Bob Silverness, e-mail message to author, February 28, 2012.

14. Steven Strieker, e-mail message to author, November 27, 2011.

15. Stocks, "Online Course Postings."

16. Mary Alice Anderson, student interviews, Winona Area Learning Center, Winona, Minnesota, April 7, 2012.

17. Sarah Priem, "Winona Mural in the Making at WALC," *Winona Post*, February 12, 2012, www.winonapost.com/stock/functions/VDG_Pub/detail.php?choice=46242&home _page=&archives=1.

18. Susan Ballje. Phone conversation and e-mail message to author, February 16 and 17, 2012, *Bay View Historical Society*. The text is also available at the Bay View Historical Society Website, www.bayviewhistoricalsociety.org/educational-initiatives.

19. L. J. Bates, "Old Abe the Battle Eagle," *Alfred Whital Stern Collection of Lincolniana*, Library of Congress, http://hdl.loc.gov/loc.rbc/lprbscsm.scsm0174.

20. Robin Vogt, "Online Course Postings: Teaching with Primary Sources," comment, University of Wisconsin–Stout, August 5, 2011, https://uwstout.courses.wisconsin.edu/d2l/home.

## BIBLIOGRAPHY

Anderson, Mary Alice. "Making Local History Live: A Collaborative Project with a Technology Base." *Multimedia & Internet @ Schools* 10, No. 5 (October 2003): 22–23.

———. "Geocaching for Fun and Learning." *Multimedia & Internet @ Schools* 15, no. 2 (March/ April 2008): 32–35.

*Bird's Eye View of Canon City, Colo. County Seat of Fremont County 1882. [By] H. Wellge. Beck & Pauli, Lithographers*. Digital image. Library of Congress Geography and Map Division. http://hdl.loc.gov/loc.gmd/g4314c.pm000560.

"The Branding of America—For Teachers." Library of Congress. www.loc.gov/teachers/ classroommaterials/presentationsandactivities/presentations/branding.

"Browse Collections by Topic." *American Memory* from the Library of Congress. Accessed March 31, 2012. http://memory.loc.gov/ammem/index.html.

"Historic American Newspapers—Chronicling America." *Historic American Newspapers*. Library of Congress. http://chroniclingamerica.loc.gov.

*Interior View, Basement, Looking Southwest at the Gear Pit below the Grinding Stones, Showing Wooden Cogs Attached to Underground Turbines—Schech's Mill, Beaver Creek State Park, La Crescent, Houston County, MN*. Digital image. Library of Congress Prints and Photographs Division. www.loc.gov/pictures/item/mn0206.photos.091391p.

Kelsey, Marie. "Saving School and Community History: The Hermantown High School Archival Project." *Minnesota Media* (2003): 34–36. www.hermantown.k12.mn.us/high/Library _Archives.

Lee, Russell. *Pilot Stepping from Pilot Boat to Dock, Pilottown, Louisiana*. Digital image. Library of Congress Prints and Photographs Division. www.loc.gov/pictures/item/fsa1997024313/ PP.

"Lessons and Corresponding K–6 Reading Standards." Winona County Historical Society Activities. 2011. www.winonahistory.org/wordpress/wp-content/uploads/Winona -County-History-Curriculum1.pdf.

McQuaid, Monica. "History Project." Agrirama: Georgia's Official Museum of Agriculture. August 22, 2010. http://mon111.edu.glogster.com/history-project.

Moore, Isaac W. *The Eagle Map of the United States*. Digital image. Library of Congress Geography and Map Division. http://hdl.loc.gov/loc.gmd/g3700.np000151.

"The National Curriculum Standards for Social Studies: A Framework for Teaching Learning and Assessment." *NCSS Bulletin* 111 (2010).

"National Education Technology Plan 2010." US Department of Education. www.ed.gov/technology/netp-2010.

New York State Department of Education. *Social Studies Core Curriculum*. www.p12.nysed.gov/ciai/socst/pub/sscore1.pdf.

*Nome City, Sept. 21, '99, a City Two Months Old*. Digital image. Panoramic Photographs (Library of Congress). September 21, 1899. http://memory.loc.gov/ammem/collections/panoramic_photo/pnnome.html.

*"Old Abe the Battle Eagle" Song & Chorus Poetry by L. J. Bates, Esq.; Music by T. Martin Towne, Author of* Our Boys Are Coming Home. Digital image. Library of Congress, Rare Book and Special Collections Division. http://hdl.loc.gov/loc.rbc/lprbscsm.scsm0174.

Priem, Sarah. "Winona Mural in the Making at WALC." Winona Post, February 12, 2012. www.winonapost.com/stock/functions/VDG_Pub/detail.php?choice=46242&home_page=&archives=1.

"Reading Standards for Literacy in History/Social Studies 6–12." *Common Core State Standards for English Language Arts & Literacy in History/Social Studies, Science, and Technical Subjects*. www.corestandards.org/assets/CCSSI_ELA%20Standards.pdf.

"Search by Standards—For Teachers." Library of Congress. www.loc.gov/teachers/standards/index.php.

Smetanka, Mary Jane. "A State Full of History and People to Tell It." *Star Tribune* (Minneapolis), December 10, 2010, www.startribune.com/local/west/111704679.html.

US Department of Education. *National Education Technology Plan 2010*. Publication. www.ed.gov/technology/netp-2010.

"Winona Newspaper Project Presented by the Winona State University Darrell W. Krueger Library." Winona State University. www.winona.edu/library/databases/winonanewspaperproject.htm.

Wolcott, Dorothy. *Young Neighbor (Julia Fletcher) of Frank H. Shurtleff Gathering from Sugar Trees for Making Maple Syrup*. Digital image. Library of Congress Prints and Photographs Division. www.loc.gov/pictures/item/fsa1998014927/PPW

# *About the Author and Contributors*

**KATHARINE LEHMAN** (editor; chapters 3 and 4) is a National Board–certified school librarian at Thomas Dale High School in Chester, Virginia, where she was Teacher of the Year in 2009. She received her MSLS from Southern Connecticut State University. She has taught adjunct classes in library science at Old Dominion University and Longwood University. She is past president of the Virginia Educational Media Association. Her publications include articles in Knowledge Quest, Teacher Librarian, and Library Media Collection. She coauthored *Power Researchers: Transforming Student Library Aides into Action Learners* (Libraries Unlimited, 2011), a curriculum guide, with Lori Donovan. Lehman has served on the Library of Congress Professional Review Committee for the TPS Direct program (Teaching with Primary Sources) since its inception. She attended the Library of Congress Summer Institute in 2011.

The talented contributors in this book are presenters and participants of the Summer Institute or members of the TPS Review Committee that Katharine Lehman invited to participate in this project.

**MARY ALICE ANDERSON** (chapter 5) is an online instructor for the School of Education, University of Wisconsin–Stout, where she teaches Digital Classroom: Teaching with Primary Sources. She also teaches for the Library Media Education Department at Minnesota State University–Mankato. She is a member of the Library of Congress professional development curriculum review committee for K–12 educators and was an American Memory Fellow. Anderson also worked with a group that developed educator guides for the *Minnesota Reflections* primary source collections. Previously she worked as a middle school media specialist in Winona, Minnesota.

**SHARON METZGER-GALLOWAY** (chapter 1) is an Educational Resource Specialist for the Educational Outreach Department of the Library of Congress. She has coordinated the summer professional development summer institutes, created lessons and activities for the online professional development program, presented at national and international educational conferences, and authored articles for national journals. She brings the Jefferson Building to life as she leads school groups and visiting educators through the architectural features and exhibits. She is a former Teacher in Residence at the Library of Congress. Before coming to the Library, she was a middle school librarian in Clifton, Colorado, where she was awarded the Colorado Exemplary Library Media Center Program of the Year Award and the Colorado Department of Education's High Performance Colorado Power Library Media Program Award.

**BARBARA STRIPLING** (introduction) is currently an Assistant Professor of Practice in the School of Information Studies, Syracuse University. Previously in her 35-year library career, Stripling has been Director of Library Services for the New York City schools, a school library media specialist, and school district director of libraries in Arkansas, a library grant program director in Tennessee, and director of library programs at a local education fund in New York City. She received her Doctorate in Information Management from Syracuse University in May 2011 and has written or edited numerous books and articles. Stripling is a former president of the American Association of School Librarians and is the 2013–2014 President of the American Library Association.

**SARA SUITER** (chapter 2) is currently the learning services librarian at Howard Community College in Columbia, Maryland. She recently graduated from the University of North Carolina at Chapel Hill with a master of science in Library Science and earned a Certificate in International Development Policy from Duke University. She served as the 2010–2011 Library of Congress Teacher-in-Residence, working with the Educational Outreach team to help teachers incorporate the Library's digitized primary sources into high-quality instruction. Before working at the Library of Congress, Sara taught third grade at a dual-language immersion public charter school in Washington, DC.

# *Index*

Locators in *italic* refer to figures/tables
LOC = Library of Congress